I Married Japan

Japan's Hilarious Journey
Into One Man's Life

William M. Dean

WMDbooks

ISBN: 1522891803
ISBN-13: 978-1522891802

Printed in the United States of America.

WMDbooks rev. date: Mar 12, 2016

For

Junko

For all of your
love,
patience
and support.

And, for never a dull day!

CONTENTS

ACKNOWLEDGMENTS

With thanks to my parents who always believed I'd be a writer in spite of the evidence.

And thank you to my siblings who have always supported my artistic efforts, even after it became apparent that I am unlikely to become rich and famous, and hitching their wagon to my star was a sure way to end up needing a tow.

And, of course, a great big thank you to my wife, Junko, and children, Noah and Rihana, who suffered my absences in silence, often drowning their misery in hollow shopping, dining and box office experiences whenever I disappeared to shape other worlds, alone, in my office. Thank you, also, for believing in me and in my claim that time on Facebook is an important part of being a writer.

And finally, thank you Japan for being so not-Western, and for my wife.

INTRODUCTION

In 2003 I married a Japanese woman who probably wishes she did not inspire me to write so much about her and her family. Her name is Junko, and I find her to be as strange and interesting as her native country.

Obviously, with her in my life, Japan also became a large element of my daily existence. Over the years, I have struggled to understand the Japanese language, the people, and my wife and have proved inept in all three subjects. However, the struggle has been entertaining.

This book is a collection of humorous articles about Japan, and the Japanese in my life. I have been careful not to discard accuracy for laughs. What you will read is all real, all happened to me, and the essential facts of the experiences are intact.

ABOUT THIS BOOK

The first half of *I Married Japan* contains stand-alone articles on various aspects of Japan in my life. The second half is a travelogue of the adventure in bringing my parents to visit Japan, in early 2015.

I have included photos, reproduced in living black and white. If you want to see the full color versions, plus a few extra photos not included in the book, you'll find a gallery on my book support website at: wmdbooks.com

Thank you for purchasing. I hope you enjoy the experience.

CHAPTER 1

A Marriage Made in Japan

My wife, Junko is an import. She's Asian; Japanese, to be specific.

Sometimes, our differences make life extra fun. Sometimes, not so much.

I keep a list of words that Junko has trouble saying; rural, juror, refractions, reflection. And, for a while I insisted the name of our first-born be Lilith, just because she couldn't pronounce it, and it would be fun watching her friends and family try. Junko vetoed this idea. The fact that our first-born was a boy was also a factor.

On balance, Junko has an entire dictionary filled with words that I can't pronounce. For instance, *doitachimashite* (you're welcome), *atatakakata* (it was hot), *ikitakunakata* (I didn't want to go).

Junko does the grocery shopping and, as a result, the inside of our fridge is like a montage of cheap horror flicks, with all the claws, scales and tentacles. It's a scary place where fish still have heads on them, as if they were once alive!

And then there's the Natto; a stinky, gooey paste made out of fermented soybeans. The last time I encountered stuff this ugly was on a bathroom floor, after a frat party. Like Haggis in Scotland, Vegemite in Australia, Millennium Eggs in China and Spam in America, it's that gastronomic bridge that only the rare outsider can cross, and the reason I always offer my wife a Tic Tac before a kiss.

To Junko this stuff is comfort food, though it generates a lot of discomfort, in me: As does seeing my wife's lips ringed with pitch-black squid ink after she's been pecking at the meal that she's preparing for me. I'm still not sure if she's a good cook or not, but she's definitely broadened my gastronomic horizons.

Food issues aside, Junko and I are very comfortable in our married life and I sometimes find it strange to think that only three years before, I was dating a blond, blue-eyed Caucasian.

How did I end up here from there?

Well, it all started, of course, with the blond and I going our separate ways.

We'd broken up and gotten back together so many times over the previous five years that I guess she felt this time, she had best pack up her horse and other worldly possessions and leave the country in order to make it stick. She moved to Oregon.

It stuck.

At about this same time, Junko was in Japan, pretty much resigned to remain there, to marry by arrangement of her family and to spend the rest of her life as a traditional Japanese wife and mother, comforted by fond memories of her adventurous globe-trotting youth. Her parents had endured four years of her wanderlust, but now forbid her to prolong this unproductive indulgence.

Junko was not happy. Conflicted by duty and desire, she did what many Japanese do in time of crisis–something she had never done before–she visited a psychic. The fortuneteller asked her name and birthday, assessed her palm and told her that she absolutely must return to Canada. Junko was startled.

The fortune-teller's advice mirrored Junko's desires but flew in the face of all she had been taught about being a good Japanese daughter and citizen. The friend who had recommended the psychic was also startled. In all the years she had been going to her, she had never been told anything so emphatically, nor had she ever been given the psychic's personal card, a token of good fortune—also, a reminder of the good karma that can come from returning to your fortune teller with a financial gift, once your good fortune has come true. It is interesting to note that, to this day, Junko has never revisited the fortune teller with a gift. Either she feels she was short changed by marrying me, or that the very fact that she never repaid her proves that the fortune teller was not good enough at predicting the future to deserve a tip.

Junko packed some bags and stowed them at a friend's house. A few days later, in the darkness of early morning, before her father rose to tend his fields of green onion, Junko snuck away, and boarded a train headed for Tokyo airport.

Because she tends to sleep late, she was half way to Canada before her family knew that she was missing. When she landed in Vancouver, the immigration officer stamped her passport granting her one more year of visiting privileges.

Meanwhile, I was suddenly, truly single again and I promised myself at least one entire year of wild and crazy, commitment-free living: Extreme singlehood!

It was because of this personal vow that my wife and I never dated before marriage.

Junko had arrived at the periphery of my life a few years before. She had a working holiday visa and started a small business wholesaling fresh sushi to the catering company that is our family business. In the one year she sold sushi to us, she made many friends—a lot of them members of my family—and after her work visa ran out, we still bumped into each other at social gatherings. I was barely aware that she had ever left the country, when I saw her again.

She was sweet and demure and I had always been attracted to her, but had never asked her out. Though I instinctively knew that Junko was the "marrying kind," I was very committed to not being committed and I also knew that her visitor's visa would expire in a few months. So, she seemed little threat to my singlehood pledge.

Junko and I started spending more time together. Whenever we went somewhere, we asked for separate bills, and I often reminded her "just so you know, this is not a date, right?" And she agreed. I'm not sure why. Perhaps she wanted nothing more than one last fling before returning home forever. Now that I know her better, I'm more inclined to believe that she was being very, very devious.

In December of 2001, her visa finally expired and Junko prepared to fly back home for the very last time. "We" would surely have ended there but for a series of last minute coincidences.

It was Christmas time, and she was going back to Japan, via Hawaii, for one last week of exotic vacation before settling back into rural Japanese life. My family was headed to Hawaii for my brother's wedding and our accommodation included one extra bed. My family all knew and liked Junko so, without asking me, they invited her along. It shouldn't be a conflict for me, they reasoned, as we hadn't been "dating." She would just be "one more friend" in the wedding party.

Coincidentally, my one "extreme single" year ended at Christmas. We finally dated—for five days. We fought for three of them. What I thought would be our last fight, turned out to be our first.

Our entire group was scheduled to depart the same day; my brother and his new wife for another week of honeymooning on another Hawaiian island, Junko for Japan, and the rest of us back home to Victoria, Canada. For convenience's sake, we spent our last night, in a hotel near the airport. Junko and I shared a room with the honeymooners, whispering our goodbyes to each other in the dark.

When it came time for us to part at the airport I felt like something very important was getting away. I felt sad and empty. But I couldn't commit to her based on our short history, so I waved goodbye.

Junko did the same, but showed no emotion. Very Japanese.

I had promised to call her, so I did.

We were in the early stages of a blossoming love, but without the dating history to justify it. Strange territory. Stranger still, for Junko. She was over twenty-five years old and unmarried. In Japan, that made her an "old maid." The Japanese refer to them as "Christmas cake;" something that everyone wants before the twenty-fifth, but is difficult to give away on the twenty-sixth.

Her relatives were anxious to arrange a marriage for her. Her aunt's friend's son had seen Junko's picture and accepted a marriage meeting at Junko's earliest convenience. He was young, handsome and well-off. The family was excited and relieved.

Junko was depressed.

She could not tell anyone that her hopes, her heart, lay with a noncommittal *Hakujin* (Caucasian) man she had only "officially" dated for less than a week. She lived with her parents, did her chores, looked for a job—searched for some way out of the servant life of a spinster, some escape plan that did not include marrying for convenience, rather than love.

4

Our phone conversations were not joy filled. Junko tried, but couldn't get a job. The work-culture in Japan is different from here, and so are the hiring laws. She is well educated and when she was younger, she had found several very good, high-paying jobs. But now, prospective employers skimmed her resume and asked only, "Why, are you not married? Why, don't you have children?"

In Japan, it is commonly understood that by the age of thirty, a woman should be married and at home raising children and making a good home for her husband, not out getting a job. More than just a cultural issue, it's also good business practice: Younger girls cost less than older, experienced workers. She watched as interviewer after interviewer took her resume, drew a bold red circle around her age, then pointedly placed it atop the pile of other red-circled resumes, obviously destined for the trash.

Each day, the pressure from her concerned family mounted. Junko stayed silent, confiding only to one special aunt. She put on a brave face, tried to keep her situation from influencing me when we talked on the phone, all the while desperately hoping that I would travel to Japan, meet her family, sweep her away to Canada; marry her.

In May, I went to Japan.

After fifteen hours of travel I was tired and looking forward to freshening up. Junko promised that I would love her family's bath and filled me with thoughts of a long, hot spa-like soak. One of the many ways in which Japanese bathrooms are different from Western ones is the bathtub. Japanese ones are luxurious—long and deep, the water temperature automatically maintained. They are made for lounging, relaxing. Showers are for washing.

But my soap-bubble dream quickly burst. As I said, the Japanese bath is not for washing. Japanese families share the bath water. Traditionally, the father goes first, followed by the eldest son, youngest son, mother, eldest daughter and so on. The father may allow an honored guest to bathe first. The lowest-ranking person goes last. As a foreign stranger intent on stealing away his only daughter, I would probably rank lower than the family dog. I opted for a quick shower.

My room couldn't have been any more authentically Japanese;

paper walls, tatami mats underfoot, a futon as a bed. In the morning, I was awakened by the giggles of children. It was Junko's nephews; Kazuki who was nine and Hiroki, seven. Two diminutive silhouettes slipped along the paper walls of the hallway, then dark eyes peered in through rips in the paper. I sat up in bed and their eyes became saucers. They had never seen a Caucasian in the flesh and they had never imagined them to be so hairy. Hiroki asked his mother if he could take me to school for show and tell. She said no.

Junko slept late, as was her habit, and none of Junko's family spoke English, so breakfast was pretty quiet. Her father was polite, but distant, and quickly left to tend his green onion fields leaving instructions to try and keep me in the yard. He didn't want all the neighbors talking. Junko's mother fussed to make me something I recognized. I had a piece of dry toast.

Junko and I quickly realized that if we wanted more time together she would have to come back to Canada so that we could explore our connection. But this was such a strange, noncommittal situation that there was no hope of explaining it to her family. She did her best impression of a stereotypicalyl stoic Japanese, answered her parents' questions in one word or less, offered nothing. When her father attempted to interview me using her as interpreter, she severely edited my answers, altered them entirely, I suspect. She didn't want them to know that I was merely a part-time caterer, that I write unpublished novels, that I was divorced, that we were not committed, let alone engaged. There was nothing redeemable in my present circumstances, it seemed. The only real communication between her father and I was through eye contact. And I could tell that despite Junko's best efforts, he knew or suspected all our secrets.

I spent most days reading novels on a sunlit boulder amid bonsai-like shrubs in the Japanese garden, or playing with the nephews who were still fascinated by me; my strange skin, my hairy body, my inability to speak their language. They brought friends around to see me. I felt a little like a sideshow exhibit. "Step right up and see the round-eyed stranger! You've never seen a living man so white! Witness the hairy forearms. Witness the towering nose. Witness the deepset eyes. Marvel at his inept pronunciation of simple words!"

After one week, her father told Junko that he thought it would be ok if I was seen beyond the garden walls. Junko and I toured the rural neighborhood, her father's fields, her ancestor's burial shrine. We went to the hardware store, and I fixed the hinges on a kitchen cabinet door. A few days later, her father let me help him plant the first rice seedlings. It was not hard work, but went much faster with two and he thanked me. That night, at dinner, we shared a bottle of beer. Somehow, through only observation and eye contact, he had taken stock of me and judged me somewhat-less-than-evil.

When it came time for us to leave, he drove us to the train station, became quiet as we hoisted our suitcases. He shook my hand, hugged his only daughter, turned away when tears began.

Junko and I lived together and finally "dated" until the next February when she accepted my marriage proposal. We were married in my parent's garden, in Victoria, on a sunny day in June of 2003 during the height of the SARs epidemic which prevented her family from attending. But that's a whole other story.

Fifteen years later: Junko, Bill, Rihana and Noah.

CHAPTER 2

That Unspoken Japanese Word

Mokusatsu —suru, v. take no notice of; treat (anything) with silent contempt; ignore [by keeping silent]; remain in a wise and masterly inactivity. Kenkyusha's New Japanese-English Dictionary. P. 1129.

"My wife is Japanese."

This is a very handy phrase that I use whenever the children say something inappropriate or I buy something with coupons.

I think it has become my personal tag line. It frames the beginning of so many of my misadventures; often starting with miscommunication, morphing into misunderstanding and finally ending in missed my head by three inches. Of course it also frames many wonderful adventures, but I don't generally write about my sex life.

One thing that many Japanese do, is communicate via silence. They have a name for it: "mokusatsu." Literally: death by silence. The idea behind it is to allow time to dissolve awkward or unpleasant issues. The most generous interpretation is: "Waiting for wisdom before speaking." But there are many connotations, running the gamut to the dismissive: "Waiting until there is something worth talking about."

Recently, I came across several articles documenting how this cultural affectation contributed to the atomic bombings at Hiroshima and Nagasaki. In July of 1945, the allies sent an ultimatum to the Japanese government. It read as follows:

"We call upon the government of Japan to proclaim now the unconditional surrender of all Japanese armed forces, and to provide proper and adequate assurances of their good faith in such action. The alternative for Japan is prompt and utter destruction."

The Japanese imagined they were debating an invasion of troops and were divided on the subject. The military and its supporters were strongly opposed to a surrender, but others were strongly in favor. Prime Minister Suzuki, it is said, favored surrender but was sandwiched between powerful and opposing forces, within his own government. It is thought that he sought to appease both sides and slowly tease out a consensus. His official reply was: "No comment."

Mokusatsu. But which connotation?

In Japan, it is popularly reported, the government and the population both felt that they were still in negotiations. In their view, the answer was clearly: "We're thinking it over."

Ten days later, a nuclear bomb obliterated Hiroshima.

It is a sad chapter in the military and cultural history of both Japan and the USA.

But, decades later, echoes of this scenario used to repeat themselves regularly, at my house. Tourists still come by to take selfies next to the craters.

My wife is an extreme practitioner of mokusatsu and it frustrated me, for years.

But then I realized that without numbers you cannot talk mathematics. Without Latin, you cannot talk medicine. Without bureaucratic jargon, you cannot talk with government. And, without the proper Japanese vocabulary, you cannot communicate properly to a Japanese person.

I have studied Japanese, and learned enough to make the kids laugh whenever I attempt to speak it but I had never been taught that one, most important and unspoken Japanese word: Silence.

And now that I have learned it, you'd think I could start filling in those craters.

But, being stubborn and verbose, I still don't always accept silence as an answer. Foolishness like that will run you smack into another interesting Japanese cultural norm: beating around the bush. This follows from a centuries-long societal love affair with politeness and propriety. The Japanese prefer to talk around a problem without stating anything that might possibly be offensive, or awkward—most especially, if it regards feelings. It's a tricky skill to master; almost an art form. And, just to elevate it to an Olympic event; what they consider potentially offensive can be as small as: "Jam or jelly?" To function efficiently among the Japanese, one must learn to make, what might seem to us, great leaps of deductive reasoning.

When my Japanese wife says...

• "Maybe." That's an emphatic "No!"

• "What would you like for dinner?" means: She's not hungry. Make yourself a sandwich.

• "No problem." It's a problem.

• If we're wandering through a furniture store and she says, offhandedly, "I kind of like that book shelf." It means that the bookshelf that I hand crafted six months ago for the kids room was the wrong color, size, shape or style; at any rate, wholly inadequate and possibly offensive and next time buy one that looks like this one.

I was once gifted two weeks of stony silence because when she said, "The sun is melting the butter," I put the butter in the fridge instead of getting a new blind for the kitchen window.

Often, I have no idea why she has gone silent and I've learned not to ask. Asking only deepens the offense because if you have to ask, you haven't been paying attention. I only find out on those rare occasions when she totally loses it—usually over something extremely trivial and completely unrelated.

ME: "I picked up a new shower curtain, like you asked."

JUNKO: "How much?"

ME: "I got the next-to-cheapest: $6.99"

JUNKO: "Why didn't you just get the $1.99 one? Now I will have to clean it four times before we can throw it away! Why do you always get the wrong thing?"

ME: "But, yesterday I got bread. I thought that went well..."

JUNKO: "This is just like that ugly milk crate bookshelf in the kid's room..."

A-a-and there it is.

So, to recap: Getting a Japanese person to express an explicit opinion can really only be achieved by marrying them, then making them extremely angry.

If only we'd known all of this in 1945—or, really, any time before I built that bookshelf.

CHAPTER 3

The True Artists In My House

My house has artists the way others have silverfish. My kids are mini art-factories, pumping out scraps that become priceless masterpieces once they scrawl the words "I Love you Daddy." The "I Love you Mommy" pieces are also valuable, but less creative, as I consider these non-fiction.

I spend a lot of time pumping words into novels and blogs hoping to create masterpieces without having to resort to kissing up to my parents.

And then there's my wife, Junko.

The other day I stood watching her dissect a head of lettuce so that she could individually wash each leaf before preparing a salad and a couple of thoughts passed through my brain much in the same way that light doesn't. First: The disquieting notion that my wife was smiling while dissecting a head. This was immediately followed by the thought that I eat a lot less bugs than the average person.

According to the first article in the list after Google performed an exhaustive search, the average person consumes between one and two pounds of bugs, per year. This means that, by now, I would have eaten my wife's weight in bugs had she not been preparing most of my meals, for the last 12 years. As it is, I have consumed one and a half of my children's weight. Why I see this in terms of how many of my family members I have eaten, I do not know. Suffice it to say, I am a survivor and you do not want to go down in a plane in the Andes, with me aboard.

Once, when we were dating, I took Junko to a fancy local restaurant, whose name I will decline to mention. Actually, my memory is a bit foggy on this detail. It may have been another fancy restaurant whose name I will decline to mention. Yes... more likely there. At any rate, as we tucked into our first course, I noticed a small pile of black dots accumulating at the edge of Junko's salad plate.

ME: "Are those peppercorns?"

JUNKO: "Bugs."

ME: "Wha-a-at? There can't be bugs in a salad from a restaurant as fine as this one which I will decline to mention the name of."

JUNKO: "Actually, I've never had a salad in a restaurant which did not contain a bug."

ME *(checking over both shoulders, leaning forward and whispering, conspiratorially)*: "Do you think it's because you're Japanese?"

Junko pressed her lips thin and gave me that look: The one that asks, "Are you four?" It made me simultaneously feel foolish and proud to be a Canadian.

ME: "Well it's just that I've never had a bug in a salad. Ever."

JUNKO: "You just ate one a few minutes ago. And last week, at that other restaurant that you always decline to mention the name of, I saw you eat several."

I flip another leaf and sure enough, there's a little black beetle swimming in Balsamic and goat cheese, with a touch of ginger and honey. When I say "swimming," I mean dead.

ME: "Why didn't you say something?"

Twelve years of marriage later, I can answer that question. I have come to realize that, for Junko, my suffering is an endless source of amusement. Being Japanese, Junko has made a lot of meals that elicited my "Who ate this first?" response but I set myself a strict policy to try everything at least once, before declaring it unfit for my consumption.

The first time she served fresh water eel I made myself eat every last scrap even though I thought it tasted like rancid worm rectum. I hate rancid worm rectum. When I looked up from my plate, I noticed that Junko had eaten everything except the eel. I asked her if she was saving it for last. She said, "I think it's off." When I asked her how she could silently watch me choke down an entire fish without mentioning this, she giggled.

Once, when I had an ingrown hair she offered to pluck it, noting that she plucks her body hair all the time and assuring me that I would hardly feel it. She tweezed the offender and tore the entire inner lining from my left nostril. My eyes watered and I dance around the house, screaming into my fist for about 20 minutes. She laughed for an hour and encouraged the kids to join in.

To be fair, she also laughs when she hurts herself. Still, it's weird.

If everyone were like this, standup comedy would be radically different, and involve a hammer.

When I look around our house at the few things that she keeps out for display, I am reminded of all of my treasures, which she has carefully packed into boxes for display in our attic. Admittedly, the house looks a lot better than my bachelor pad—though I do miss my boobie beer stein and Kirk and Spock salt and peppershakers.

I am the conservative, even-tempered, straight-arrow type who might just as easily have become a chartered accountant living in obscurity, as a writer living in obscurity. And now, as I stand watching Junko scrub each lettuce leaf then pat them dry with a towel I realize that, of the two of us, clearly, she is more the true artist, currently applying her talents to the fading art of homemaking.

CHAPTER 4

Gambling In Japan

Episode 1: The Blunderdome

I have no idea how it came to be that I, alone, accompanied my Japanese father-in-law to his favorite gambling facility. It was my first trip to Japan and my ignorance of the language had, basically, reduced me to the dependency-level of a two-year-old, and two-year-olds don't question adults. My wife led me to my father-in-law's car, buckled me in, shut the door and waved goodbye. The next thing I knew we were cruising down the highway thinking of all the questions we had for each other, but trying to enjoy the awkward silence.

My father-in-law (whom we now refer to as "Jisan" because this is how our kids pronounced the Japanese word for Grandfather) is a small, energetic, smiley man. He is 75 years old and a very successful farmer who owns a lot of land and still rises with the sun to work his fields. Because of the language barrier, I still know little about him except that he seems extremely kind and patient and I like that he smiles at me so much, though I suspect it's because I amuse him much in the same way a chimp would, dressed in a business suit. He often attempts to talk to me and, left on our own, we have, on occasion, actually conversed—or at least shared the illusion.

Jisan has visited us, in Canada, twice. One time, as we all sat around the dinner table at my parents' house, Jisan and I had a relatively lengthy exchange. I remember feeling my parents flush with pride and wonder as I interpreted and responded to Jisan in his native language. Afterward, there was a brief silence which my wife, Junko, tactfully ended with a fit of giggles. After drying tears of laughter, she recited our conversation. Jisan had been talking about Junko's nature when she was a child. Apparently, she often got angry and ranted. (I don't think much has changed, except that, perhaps, marriage to me has provided her good reason.) I misinterpreted and thought he was talking about relationships in general. We both contributed several sentences to the conversation; he on Junko as a child and I, my lofty thoughts on relationships, translated into Japanese baby talk. Finally, I said something profound regarding sheep nipples and Jisan furrowed his brow and chose not to comment, which ended the conversation.

From this I have deduced that the problem with me communicating in Japanese, is Junko.

On the road trip toward gambling, we conversed once again. I think he said the weather looks bad. And I agreed, even though it was a clear and sunny day. He talks weird like that, sometimes.

The gambling center was a gymnasium-sized concrete arena which I have since dubbed, The Blunderdome. It could seat hundreds on bleacher-style benches and the walls were lined with giant TV screens, each showing a different race: horses, bicycles, dogs, motorcycles and powerboats, beamed in from various locations across Japan. Other screens posted statistics and odds.

I had no clue what was going on. Jisan thrust a betting form into my hand and encouraged me to take part. I hate gambling. This is probably because I hate losing. I especially hate losing money, which just seems to me to add insult to injury.

The only other time I had ever seriously gambled was about 20 years previous when the company I worked for at that time, sent a co-worker and me, for seven days, to the Computer Electronics Show, in Las Vegas. The guy who went with me was a newly married, born-again Christian who did not gamble, drink, dance, attend live shows, flirt with women, or smile. That last one probably being the result of the others, or possible just marriage. If you were such a person and you were in Vegas at that time, then you basically sat in your room alone watching Donny and Marie while your roommate went off participating in most of those activities while trying to avoid marriage. Two days in, we had finished exploring the CES and still had five days left to burn. Eventually, I got so bored that I started playing Blackjack.

I am not much of a card player, but I guess to balance out my bad luck in roommates, life allowed me to win about $900 in the space of 3 hours. I tipped the dealer $50 and spent the remaining four days in a drunken stupor. I lost my last dollar in an airport slot machine, on our way home.

For me, the biggest lesson in all of this was that playing for money is stressful. I had to use so much of my brain that it ruled out calling it recreation. In the end, I really didn't think the $300 per hour was worth it.

I have always valued my time more than seems justified. This may be a writer-thing. We want to be writing so badly, that things like jobs, government forms, long-winded people and going to the bathroom seem to be time-wasters and we want to be highly compensated for the loss. To me, my best efforts are worth more than the $300 per hour I made playing Blackjack. Because of this feeling, I don't give every activity my best effort. Sometimes I feel sorry for my day-job employers. But, hey, you get what you pay for.

After Jisan handed me that betting form, a feeling of intense pressure descended upon me. I simultaneously did not want to gamble, and yet *did* want to win big and impress my new father-in-law. I sat quietly and began scouring the statistics, hoping that six years of University math (no matter it was a four year program) might make up for having not a single inkling about gambling, and my inability to read Japanese.

We were there for about three hours and, occasionally, Jisan came over and prodded me to place a bet. I'd go over my calculations and shake my head. Not yet ready. He smiled and returned to his own game. Eventually, the entire backside of my betting form was a scrawl of complex mathematical formulas and I went to him and said that I'd like to place a bet in the amount that I had indicated on the sheet. He examined the form, smiled, scratched his head then asked if I was sure that I wanted to wager that amount. I remained firm. He chuckled, shrugged and led me to the wicket. At the wicket a Japanese woman took my form and my money and gave me a chit. She also chuckled and may have shrugged.

I want to reiterate that this was my first trip to Japan and beyond an inability to speak the language, I had not fully mastered the simple fact that one Yen is pretty much the equivalent of one penny. After hours of calculating and fretting, I thought I would boldly wager about twenty American dollars. In actual fact, I had bet the grand sum of two dollars. University mathematics are overrated.

At any rate, I did what most gamblers do; waited anxiously, watched the race, cheered and felt flush with unjustified hope, had that hope dashed against the rocks and tore up my chit.

Having fallen $302 short of the $300 per hour mark, I was now determined to double down and redeem my hours of patient scrutinizing and calculating—not to mention my University education—but as I headed toward the wicket, Jisan gently placed a hand on my shoulder and steered me away, toward the exit gates. At this point, I still believed I had wagered at least $20 and now worried that it might have been $200 and that this was an intervention. But then I noticed that everyone else was also headed for the door. The Blunderdome was closing for the day.

My father-in-law has not taken me gambling since, which is a great relief to us both. He jokes that he's waiting until the next time I have 200 Yen burning a hole in my pocket.

* * *

Episode 2: Pachinko

To say that I have played Pachinko is a bit like referring to a game of peek-a-boo as a manhunt.

Pachinko is played in noisy, crowded, smoke-filled Pachinko parlors reminiscent of old Las Vegas. Basic Pachinko is very similar to Pinball. You press a button which shoots little metal balls down a series of obstructions while praying that, somehow, they score points. Though you seem to have no control over the direction or velocity of these balls, it has been very convincingly demonstrated to me that there is some skill in the launching. I think it involves "chi." If you do well, the balls accumulate. If you do poorly, they disappear into the bowels of the machine. Like modern slot machines, modern Pachinko machines have lights, bells, buzzers and computer animation flashing, ringing, buzzing and frolicking about while you perform the seemingly simple, physical task of pressing the launch button. Depending upon what occurs on the background screen, you may get bonus balls or have your balls viciously devoured by the machine. And, honestly, that's just about how it feels when you quickly and continually lose at such a simple game.

Foreigners, like myself, who cannot read Kanji have absolutely no clue why Hello Kitty has suddenly appeared dancing and smiling and ripping the beating heart out of Sailor Moon, and whether or not this is a good thing and thus have no ability to strategize the pressing of that little launch button. Add the cloying heat, the cacophony, the perpetual haze of cigarette smoke and lights flashing in your eyes and you have the relaxing ambiance of a Guantanamo interrogation.

It is illegal to play Pachinko for money in Japan so, at the end, you can humbly take what's left of your balls to the gift counter and exchange them for gifts ranging from the miniscule (a pen) to the grand (an iPod or bicycle) which you can then take away. Or you can get a chit for that gift and trundle around the corner to a store owned by the same company and housed in the same building but which is somehow sufficiently arms length that they can exchange that chit for cash.

One day, Junko's family took me to a Pachinko parlor; largely, I think, because I had no idea how to say, "I really dislike gambling," in Japanese. I spent about three hours planted in front of a machine trying desperately to piece together modern Pachinko from first principles. Family members regularly came by, slapped me on the back, blew smoke in my face and said something encouraging but unintelligible then dumped extra balls into my tray to keep me going. I had no idea that they were actually pouring hundreds of dollars toward my doomed campaign.

It was only after gathering my miserable little balls in my hand and timidly proceeding to the gift counter that I realized the value. I had my pick of a sushi-shaped eraser or a small package of firecrackers. In my finest Japanese, I said, "I'll have the firecrackers, please." And that's how I came to possess a sushi-shaped eraser.

Here's a gambling tip for you: When you can't even win at the gift counter, you know that you're not cut out to play Pachinko.

CHAPTER 5

Screwed!
(When holiday traditions go awry.)

Inside the drum of my clothes dryer there are, now, six empty screw holes. After reading this article, if you ever see six empty screw holes inside of your clothes dryer, you will know what I now know:

1) that there should be a screw in each of those holes,
2) that your dryer is broken, and
3) that three hours are about to be blown out of the water.
   (This does not include time spent swearing at inanimate objects or bandaging cuts from razor-sharp metal edges.)

My wife, Junko, is Japanese* and Christmas is not really celebrated, in Japan. There, New Year's Day is the big deal. The Japanese idea is that you want to enter the new year, the way you'd like it to proceed. To me this suggests her in lingerie and me in a bottle of scotch. To Junko, it suggests sterilization—thankfully, not in the way you're thinking.

On the 31st of December all Japanese "celebrate" by rigorously cleaning everything in sight. At least that's what Junko told me and what I believed until the year we spent Christmas in Japan. That's

---

* *"My wife is Japanese" is a very useful catch-all sentence. I use it when one of the kids does something inappropriate or when I pay with coupons. If your wife is Japanese, you should use it, too. It's one of the perks.*

when I learned that my wife is a cleaning fanatic, even by Japanese standards. She'd scrub the white off of rice, if she could, and does not consider a window to be truly clean until birds start bouncing off of it.

On the 31st, we would clean the house from top to bottom, armed with old toothbrushes, razor blades, screwdrivers and crowbars, for those hard to reach spaces. We moved fridges and stoves and took apart things like shelves and small appliances to get at the nooks and crannies. Another tradition we had was that every year, after about 5 hours of this, I got grumpy and quit.

Tired and grumpy was how I entered the new year. Junko entered it disappointed and unsatisfied. And, too often, the year would proceed the way we entered it.

On that eye-opening New Year's Eve when we were in Japan, her father spent a couple of hours tidying up and leisurely organizing his tools in the garage. He whistled a lot. Her sister-in-law was humming like a princess in a Disney movie, as she lightly dusted the furniture. My two teenaged nephews brushed their teeth, then watched TV. They laughed and laughed. There was no grunting, groaning or muttering of curses, and the rest of the day was spent lounging and visiting with friends. The jig was up!

Junko has since scaled down my New Year's Eve chores to only a couple of hours' work. I insist on a list in advance, so that I know what I'm up against. Sometimes, I will start a few days ahead in order not to spoil my holiday. This year, my list included cleaning the dryer of all lint. Junko had noticed that lint was gathering in behind the drum. She also noted that there were six screws that appeared to offer access to that area in order to clean it.

I want to take a moment to point out that I am actually quite handy. I build stuff, can change my own brakes and oil, have repaired everything from vacuum cleaners to furnaces and done a lot of renovating, and none of that has ever taken a nasty turn.

In this case, however, I was lulled into a false sense of security by the prevalent, modern notion that evolution is going about it all wrong and that being a moron should not lead to harm. The 6-inch deep, blow-up kiddie pool I bought last summer has a warning label: "No Diving", and our toaster's manual advises users not to butter the bread before it's toasted.* Naturally, I assumed that screws so visible and accessible were meant to be removed.

A distant voice inside my head was telling me that this was a bad idea, but I ignored it thinking that it was just the ghost of resentment at having chores on my holiday. I figured, the worst-case scenario might be a wasted minute or two. What the voice was trying to say was that even if I removed the screws, it is obvious that the panel cannot be removed because the dryer vanes are in the way and this should be a warning that those screws are not meant to be removed. But they were so accessible and invitingly shiny! And the voice was all whiny and condescending.

When the first screw came free, I immediately sensed that something heavy had shifted. I have no idea why I carried on. I am normally the most cautious guy in the world. When I'm not sure how something is going to pan out, it is my policy to do nothing. This is why I don't play the lottery and, by extension, why I must waste precious holiday-time tampering with a dryer.

Removing the second screw had no effect. But when that third screw came out, a large metal disc behind the drum fell onto the heating element. The coils glowed fiercely for a few seconds, then shorted out with a blinding flash and a crisp pop. They were now broken and welded to the rest of the dryer. My wife pointed out that we were lucky that I, too, had not been welded to the dryer. She was probably concerned for my well being, but it's equally likely that she was thinking that the constant clunking sound of my body tumbling around whenever she did the laundry would eventually become tedious.

My five-minute cleaning job had just expanded to fill the day.

I am ashamed to say that I did some cursing. But, to my credit, it lasted no more than 30 minutes. Ok, an hour. But, I did not curse my wife or the dryer, itself. I cursed the engineer who designed it and who decided to place six temptingly shiny screws where I could so easily get at them. Also, all of his ancestors. Then I cursed myself for a while. That was fun.

---

* *Sadly for me, there is no warning on a package of Doritos to tell you that the pointy ends are sharp. And nowhere on the Bandaids package does it mention that they won't stick to the roof of your mouth.*

Our stacking laundry is located in a very tight closet and locked in place by shelving on one side. In order to extract the dryer, I had to remove the shelves and lift it off the washer, pull it through a doorway designed to admit anorexic field mice, single file, and gently place it on our kitchen floor in the middle of the most traveled intersection in the house; providing the only access to the kitchen, bathroom and the back door.

While I did this, my wife went online and looked up a schematic of the dryer, then asked me why I had not done that first. My mood now much enhanced, I looked over the schematic then watched a quick repair video on YouTube, which naturally led to checking out pictures of Ellie Kemper, then jokes from *The Office*.

Eventually, I began to disassemble the dryer. The kids were suddenly parched and had to get glasses of water from the kitchen. You should know that young children have nothing between the mouth and their rear ends. Internal organs and such grow in later. So, after about 30 seconds, they had to use the bathroom. This cycle was repeated repeatedly, each time with a "How's it going, Dad?" as they passed.

"Just ducky," I said, having decided that this moment was right for a lesson in the art of sarcasm. They both gave me a thumbs up, each time.

I called around for replacement parts and was fortunate enough to find a new heating element, nearby. Thirty-five dollars and another hour later, I had vacuumed every internal inch and had the whole thing back together.

It's much more difficult to lift a stacked dryer back into place because half way up, you must adjust your grip lower down on the unit. It took me another hour to place it, attach the vent, put back the shelves and replace all the useless crap that we normally store on those shelves.

"Ok. Your damned dryer's 100% lint-free, now!" I was wise enough to not say.

Incidental to this, that same morning, my wife was cleaning the fan above the stove and stripped the screw that keeps the blade in place. I made an ingenious repair involving a drill and hack saw and put it all back together. The fan now sucks perfectly, but wails like a banshee—or sings like Kate Bush, depending upon your taste in audio.

I went to the garage to get more tools and the door handle came off in my hand. I fixed this, too. We now pry the door apart with a stick.

Lately, when I go online and search DIY repair, Google automatically redirects me to a professional repair shop.

Ok, "Mr. Fixit"—
Now, can we call a plumber?

CHAPTER 6

Navigating the Japanese Bathroom
(The ultimate elimination challenge.)

I travel to Japan more often than most, and every time I do, I wash my hands with conditioner.

Is this some sort of strange Japanese tradition? I don't think so. Maybe. But for me, it's because I can't read the labels on the bottles. My Japanese wife, Junko, seems to think that I should just "know," and offers no help.

It seems obvious to me now, but not being able to read was actually one of the larger surprises in store for me when I first toured Japan. I knew that I wouldn't be able to speak, but I had assumed that I could use a pocket dictionary to puzzle out the signage in food stores, restaurants and train stations. Nope. Most everything in public is labeled in Kanji, the ancient, exotic script adopted from China, about 1500 years ago. To be able to read a Japanese newspaper, for instance, you must know 12-1600 of these characters and their multiple meanings. I knew exactly three and most unfortunately, "men's room" was not one of them. I felt like a three year old.

I was totally dependent upon Junko. And that was frustrating. Junko is not much of a talker. She's strong willed and silent and has little patience for those who will not apply themselves—which is to say, anyone who doesn't understand things she thinks are obvious—which is to say, everything Japanese.

On a shelf in my in-laws' shower room are about seven bottles with Kanji labels, which are as legible to me as the list of chemicals in a Nib. Discerning the exact contents of those bathroom bottles has proven tricky. In Japan, pink does not necessarily mean girlie and fruit-scented does not always mean shampoo. Consequently, I once washed my hair with tile and grout cleanser.

My experiences are far from unique. For most visitors, the Japanese bathroom is a source of wonder and surprise.

The biggest surprises are found in public washrooms. The public toilet often seems like a hasty afterthought, crammed awkwardly into a corner or crudely installed in a wooden riser. The shape and what it implies about the intended procedure can be a head-scratcher. Really, best to make sure all the heavy jobs are done at home.

Bathrooms in hotels and private residences are much more familiar, though no less fascinating.

A Japanese bathing room has a shower and a deep tub in a watertight, tiled room. A great idea, if you have kids. The shower is intended for washing and the tub for relaxing. A thick insulating mat covers the tub and the water is kept full and hot by a computerized heating system. The bathtub water is used by the entire family each day, and from what I'd seen was changed, maybe once a week. (In actual fact, a computer automatically refreshes the water but the tub is only drained occasionally, for cleaning. But I did not know that, then.) For me, as a foreign guest, this is situation produced many awkward moments: Like that time when I was first in line in the bath and joined by my 2-year-old son. After the bath, I had a strong suspicion that he had peed in the water. I was new to the family, back then, and embarrassed. I decided not to mention it. Really, it was all I had the vocabulary to do. My unease increased as, one by one, family members entered the little room and I heard the splish of water as they reclined into the little hot tub: father-in-law, brother-in-law, sister-in-law, nephews. Splish, sploosh, splash! That night, my wife was puzzled when I sniffed her before letting her snuggle against me. I was relieved to find that her hair smelled only like mango. I memorized that scent for my next shower.

The Japanese tend to separate their washing and eliminating areas. A hand-washing sink is often in an adjoining, but separate, room from the shower/bath room. The toilet also has its own room, however, this is often far from the wash area. This means reorganizing your habits a bit, if you are new to the system. The toilet area incorporates some clever ideas that might require a moment or two to puzzle out.

Often, on the wall near the toilet, is what looks like a little speaker system. This is not for calling for assistance, though I think that might be a practical idea in tourist areas. It's called a Sound Princess (Oto Hime) and generates pleasant sounds to mask the noise of bodily functions. I can personally attest that this is not nearly loud enough to disguise the sound of major intestinal distress and, in a typical, thin-walled Japanese house, will do nothing to relieve the awkwardness in adjoining rooms, during such an episode.

The modern Japanese toilet, itself, is a computerized and mechanized wonder which will greet you by raising it's lid invitingly, as if to say, "Welcome, Great White Haunches, I am here to answer your every elimination whim!" And I am here to tell you that it will deliver on that promise, provided you can figure out which buttons to press. If not, however, it is fully capable of a painful assault on your nether-regions.

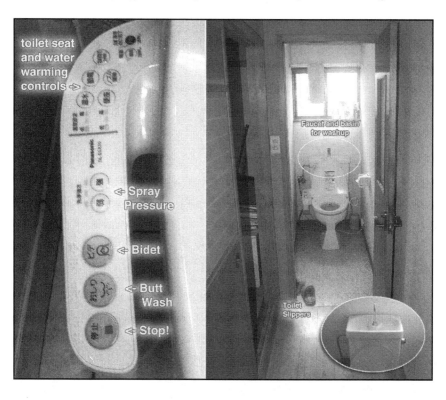

The toilet seat is usually heated and there are controls for that. Again, don't forget that Asian color scheming may not correspond to North American. Blue does not necessarily mean cold and red does not necessarily mean hot. You can't burn yourself with one of these, but my father-in-law sure yelped that Christmas when I accidentally turned off the heated seat.

The toilet seat is also equipped with a sophisticated bidet system that accurately shoots warm water precisely where cleaning is needed. You can adjust for pinpoint accuracy, however I have never had to do this. Apparently all the world shares a reasonably similar bum-structure. The temperature and pressure can be set to individual preferences—or can tear you a new one, if you fumble the controls. Again, I want to stress that, in Japan, red does not necessarily mean stop!

Like a car wash, the final stage is blow-drying. I don't believe there is a Carnauba Wax option, but I wouldn't recommend you start punching buttons at random.

Having successfully navigated the NASA-like toilet apparatus, you might be wondering where you wash your hands. Once more, the answer lies in that fancy toilet. No, not the bidet. After you flush (which on some toilets happens automatically, when you stand) and as water flows in to replenish the toilet's reservoir, it falls from a faucet into a small ceramic bowl above the tank, giving you an opportunity to lightly wash your hands. I think this is one of the more elegant ideas in the room—so clever, yet simple. The one downside with this system is that the water tends to splash a bit from the shallow bowl. If you do the North American "courtesy flush" your back will get wet. Adapt. Use the Sound Princess, instead.

One other unusual thing I've noticed is that many toilet rooms in private homes have thin doors that are primarily a large pane of frosted glass. From the outside, you only see a vague, beige blob, but I wouldn't consider it a truly private area. With walls not much thicker than cardboard, I guess the imminently practical Japanese accept that you aren't fooling anyone while you're in there.

After returning home, there may be many things you do not miss about Japan: the crowds, the pace, the cost, not being able to read, the smell of tile and grout cleanser. But one thing's for sure; you're gon'na miss that toilet.

CHAPTER 7

Dining with the Queen of England

My father was a man of few words, the majority of them shouted at the dinner table. Dinner conversation was punctuated with shotgun blasts of "Elbows off the table!", "Mouth closed when you're chewing!" and "Fork down between mouthfuls!"

I think that when my father married Mom, he thought he wanted to have kids. Then he had kids, which brought order and sanity to his world much in the same way a pet ape might, while throwing feces and pulling the limbs off relatives. Proper table manners was where he drew the line and attempted to restore order.

After we'd finish eating in silence, my siblings and I would sit rigidly in our chairs like POWs, waiting in silence for a lull in the conversation so that we could chime, "Thank-you-for-the-lovely-dinner-excuse-me-from-the-table-please" like Mary Poppins saying "supercalifragilistickexpealidocious," but much faster. Occasionally, my father would become angry at our lack of sincerity and call us back to say it again, this time, with feeling. We'd spend about a week emoting like Hamlet, then slide back into our old routine.

Dinner times were not much fun for us, back then. I survived by receding into fantasy, imagining that I was MacGyver or James Bond strapped to a chair, enduring a grueling hour of torture. My brother developed a speech impediment and my sisters chose PCs instead of Macs. However, we all are well-mannered eaters.

Since that time, I have come to see good table manners as a gift from my father. At formal dinners, I frequently notice others perplexed by seemingly extraneous utensils, confused by dining protocol and distracted by trying to eat politely. Meanwhile, for me, this is all familiar and reflexive. I am in my element, except for the lack of shouting.

I am much more lenient than Dad, but do find myself repeating his old phrases and trying to whip my kids' eating habits into shape. And whenever they ask "Why?" I answer, "You must always be prepared to dine with The Queen of England." It may well turn out that if I've taught them nothing else, I've taught them to hate Queen Elizabeth II, and possibly England, as well. If she ever did invite them for supper, they'd likely decline.

The last time we visited my wife's family in Japan, Noah was 10 and Rihana was 8. My Mom and Dad came with us on that trip, and I emphasized to the kids how strict Grampy was about table manners, so they should be on their best behavior. They rose to the occasion and the entire time Grampy was with us, I was very proud of their manners. It probably helped that there were no knives or forks, only chopsticks.

Grampy and Grammy returned home ahead of us and I breathed a sigh of relief thinking that my worries about their behavior at the table were over.

But, apparently, there was one rule I had neglected to mention.

* * *

While I was courting my Japanese wife, Junko, she was busy trying to avoid getting married to another man. Her family had arranged for her to meet and marry into a very wealthy branch of their own family. This is not uncommon in Japan: A family without heirs may adopt a full-grown outsider male to carry forward their legacy. Sometimes, to insure that he marries well, a bride is also arranged, in advance. In this case, a very rich uncle who'd had no children of his own, had chosen a young man he thought would make a suitable heir. That young man had agreed to be adopted, swapping his birth-family name for theirs. In their perfect world, my Junko would marry this man and the union would produce male children so that the family name and fortune would be secure for another couple of generations.

Because of this, Junko was reluctant to tell her parents about me. Instead, for months, she made excuses to avoid the initial marriage-meeting until, like a prince on a white stallion, I rode in on my 1975 Tercel, scooped her up and swept her away to the extravagant comforts of my musty basement suite. This is an endless source of amusement for me and whenever we can't afford to vacation in the south of France or get a tooth filled I can't help but point to that decision and laugh. We have fun together like that. If she'd married that billionaire, I doubt they would have laughed so much about such things. So, no regrets, I'm sure.

One day, for reasons that are very Japanese, Junko's father invited us all along to a business meeting with The Rich Uncle. On the way to the meeting, we preempted a possible rude moment by telling the kids to stop referring to him as "The Rich Uncle," even though that's how everyone in the family refers to him. The Rich Uncle took us on a tour of one of his warehouses, then one of his factories and then treated us to lunch. For other very-Japanese reasons, the business portion of the meeting was almost imperceptible, took under a minute and amounted to no more than three sentences. Afterward, we were invited to visit his home for a midday snack.

As might be expected, The Rich Uncle's house was a mansion; large and modern, yet with traditional elements reminiscent of a Buddhist temple. Walking through the large wooden gate felt like entering a movie set. The surrounding garden was intricate and perfect, the foyer huge and appointed with marble and exotic hardwoods. His wife (who, interestingly, is always referred to as "The Rich Uncle's Wife" and never as "The Rich Aunt") led the way down a long hallway to a large, glass-walled room that looked out on the garden. We sat on silk cushions around a massive Teak table and were served tea and expensive baked goods on very fine china. To be honest, being more familiar with plywood and brick shelving and milk crate coffee tables, I am easily impressed and have no idea whether all the elements were indeed as expensive as they looked or were purchased on roll-back at Wal-Mart. Still, the setting was convincing.

There was an extended silence as we all settled in and I was never more happy to have drilled fine dining etiquette into my children because it felt like we were actually about to dine with The Queen of England.

And that's when my darling daughter, Rihana, farted.

It was not one of those subtle, muffled farts that might have been mistaken for the rustling of clothing against silk cushions or the low resonance of a saucer scuffing across polished Teak. It was a tuba-esque performance more akin to a Mac truck giving birth to farm equipment.

All eyes turned toward Rihana.

She pointed to her brother. "It wasn't me!" she lied.

Fart, point and lie. A faux pas hat trick!

I felt my father turning over in his easy chair.

It is more difficult than you might think to act casual and snap photos of the snack food while trying to blend with the aristocracy.

CHAPTER 8

Don't Panic!
It's Only Japan.

It's a popular Internet meme that strange and Japan are synonymous. But then Donald Trump is running for President of the United States. So, who are we to judge?

Junko and I travel to Japan about every four years, and for me, all the important things are similar and only the inconsequential things are different. But, those inconsequential things can be surprising. Even though I now have a deeper understanding, a trip to Japan is still as exotic and exciting as it was the first time, and the wonder and strangeness never seem to fade.

Below, is a list of the differences that I most noticed when I first set foot in Japan. As with every other such list of peculiarities, this one will prepare you for Japan much in the same way that basting prepares the turkey to enjoy a happy Thanksgiving.

IN THE HOME:
• I was not surprised by the automated toilet seats, as their existence is now widely known. However, I was surprised how quickly I got used to it and how badly I wanted one for my own house. Ten years later, I have one and can say with confidence that only a toddler's butt could be more pampered, and, in every sense of the phrase, I have probably written much more than is justified on the Japanese toilet.

My father-in-law's rural home. Most Japanese houses still have this traditional look, however, American-style housing is becoming increasingly popular.

• Japanese toilets have a small faucet and basin above the cistern. After you flush, the incoming water is used for washing your hands.

• Slippers are a big deal. The entranceway to every home has a tiled area below floor level dedicated to the idea. You are expected to doff your shoes there and then slip into guest slippers to cross the wooden floors of the rest of the home. At the entrance to the bathroom will be yet another pair of special, rubber slippers. You back out of your guest slippers and slip into these while using the toilet. I found it arduous to change upon entering every room and eventually gave up. Being Caucasian gives you some license to ignore tradition and get away with it.

Typical entranceway in Japanese house.

• Toilet and washing up areas are separated, in most houses. This means some rearranging of daily hygiene rituals.

• The shower and bathtub are together in a waterproof room. You are expected to wash using the shower and relax in the tub. Family and guests all share the same bathwater, which is recycled, cleaned and replenished via a computerized system. The bathtub is drained periodically for cleaning, but otherwise stays full and warm, with an insulated cover over top to save energy.

• Many of the homes I've visited have both a Western-, as well as a Japanese-style, living room. In the traditional Japanese-style living room, the table stands in a square pit that has an electric heater at the bottom. The duvet-like blanket is called a *kotatsu* and is used to conserve the heat, during colder

Above: "Dad! Why are there weeds in the bathtub?" Noah asks. "We're making kid soup!" I explain. On May 5th (Children's Day) it is tradition to put Iris leaves and roots in the bathwater to promote good health and ward off evil.

Below: typical bath, washing room and laundry arrangement.

weather. In most Japanese homes, this is as close to central heating and insulation as you are going to get.

• Most Japanese homes have no insulation or central heat. The idea is to heat bodies, not rooms. In cold weather, they wear layers and eat hot foods. A lot of leisure time is spent around the Japanese living room table, your lower body huddled under the *kotatsu,* while an electric heating unit warms your toes, from below.

• You will find only cooking knives in Japanese kitchens. There are few, if any, butter knives, and nothing like a steak knife. The cook is expected to serve the meal with everything pre-sliced and diced, convenient for eating with chopsticks.

• Japanese housewives grocery shop, daily. I'm uncertain whether this is cause or effect, but Japanese households are not built for stockpiling. Fridges and cupboards are one-third the size of the American equivalent.

Japanese-style livingroom.

• In Japan, the traditional family culture is very strong and includes a stay-at-home mom. In this arrangement, the women control the purse strings and do the majority of the purchasing, so businesses have found it in their best interest to make shopping as convenient as possible for housewives with toddlers. The most obvious example is the prevalence of large, kid-oriented amusement centers in department stores. Often, they employ an attendant—or, more recently, a robot!—who will supervise the children. The price is always so reasonable that it becomes unreasonable not to utilize the service. This is quite opposite of the Western idea of charging parents through the nose for things their kids desire.

• TV: The language barrier never seems so high as when you watch Japanese television. Almost every program introduces some element that seems bizarre and requires an explanation. After a while, you just go for a walk.

Beyond a clutter of garish typewritten comments pasted over just about every show, a small box is often inset in one corner featuring the face of a celebrity guest watching the same thing that you are watching. His/her reaction to the material is meant to help you appreciate, in the proper way, the content; like a laugh-track in an American comedy. The celebrities can be seen reacting to what is on the screen which helps set the context for the audience: They laugh when it's supposed to be funny and make appropriate exclamations when something is surprising, horrific, or looks tasty.

When watching news and current-affairs programs you will notice that broadcasters still use paper charts with peel and stick

In general, areas of leisure and entertaining are relatively large and spacious, whereas areas of production like the kitchen, laundry and bathroom are designed for effeciency and tend to be cramped and cluttered.

labels as much as they use computer graphics. This reflects a long tradition of cleverly utilizing paper.

• Outdoor banks of vending machines are a common sight in every neighborhood. They may be found wherever there is power and some shelter, and are as common on rural back roads as they are on urban thoroughfares. Most dispense juice, coffee, tea and cigarettes, but I've also seen ones that sell comic books, condoms and even, one offering a variety of household objects like brushes, screwdrivers, rubber bands and light bulbs. An urban legend persists that Japanese vending machines sell used panties. This has some basis in fact: For a brief time there were a few such machines, but then new laws were made to address the disturbing practice, and those few machines disappeared.

FOOD:

• If you look up the world's 50 weirdest foods via Google, you will find that Japan corner's the market with eight contributions. The Japanese are obsessed with food and have a very broad palate. They are also obsessively polite. Consequently, "Oishi!" (tasty!) is the most commonly used Japanese word. If you say, "Here, have some three-day-old burnt Kraft Dinner I scraped from a pan I found on the side of the road...," they will take a microscopic nibble, smile and say, "Oishi!"

Japanese TV programs are... different.

• If you ever host a Japanese visitor, you need to know that they are not used to using knives to eat their meals. I realized this the first time my Japanese father-in-law visited Canada and I took him out for dinner with a group of friends and family. He does not speak English and could not read the menu, so I ordered a steak for him. I was almost finished my meal before noticing that he hadn't taken a bite of his steak. And that's when it dawned on me that in Japan, everything is served already cut, suitable for chopsticks. He had no experience wielding a knife in such a precise manner and I guess he felt too self-conscious to take a "stab" at it. I surreptitiously sliced it up for him. We were both slightly embarrassed.

• It is polite to slurp your soup. I'm so well Westernized that I was unable to do this without spraying the room with noodle drippings. The family was surprised that I lacked this basic culinary skill.

• Restaurants—including many fast food places—will give you a wet napkin to wash your hands with, before a meal. It's gauche to wash your face with this.

• Generally, restaurants do not supply paper napkins. They assume you carry tissue with you and can use that. When licking my fingers doesn't cut it, I steal the toilet paper and try to keep it hidden.

This is a popular type of inexpensive sushi restaurant referred to as kaiten-zushi, literally "rotation sushi." Customers grab whatever they want from the conveyor belts (background) and pay between one and three dollars, for each plate. The prices are indicated by the color of the plates.

• A related observation: There are no paper towels in restaurant bathrooms.

• Japanese ice cream, pizza toppings candy and potato chip flavors include things like wasabi, seaweed, squid, shrimp and corn.

• I never saw anyone eating anything while walking—not even a candy bar or a hot dog. I have since learned that it is considered rude. The Japanese always take their food somewhere, and sit to enjoy it.

• I noticed that corn seems inordinately relished, though it is a common vegetable, in Japan.

• Many things in Japan are about one-third smaller than in North America, but not beer. It's served in mugs that are about one and a half times larger than what we get here.

• FINANCE: Cash is still the most common transaction. Credit cards are still not accepted in a lot of places, even where they expect tourists. And banks still verify your identity by a personal family ink stamp, a practice I had never heard of, before I went to Japan.

• REAL ESTATE: In the rural area where I've spent most of my time, houses either look completely dilapidated or brand new. Old houses are mowed down rather than renovated. My father-in-law's 50-year-old house had been constructed from 40-foot spans of clear timber that, these days, only the wealthiest people could afford. Two years ago, that lumber was hauled away and burned before they started construction of his new house. The idea of renovating an existing structure seems to only now be gaining traction, probably due to the extended economic downturn.

• TOURISM: In cosmopolitan areas like Tokyo, the Japanese are making strides in accommodating English-speaking tourists. However, their efforts are still rudimentary and unevenly applied; mostly amounting to English signage. You may well follow English signs to a bilingual ticket agent and book a three hour guided tour only to find the guide speaks only Japanese. I would not yet say that Japan is a comfortable destination for English-speakers.

• RELAXATION: The Onsen is a traditional Japanese public bath, designed for relaxation. They are ubiquitous throughout Japan and a very common form of recreation. Onsens feature large, communal hot tubs in which people bathe naked. Men and women usually bathe in separate facilities. If you go, expect to be gawked at by Japanese children.

On my last trip, I noticed two strange things that I had never noticed before. The first thing was that, in the change room, the other men tended to cover their private parts with a small towel, even though we were all male, and all soon to be exposed.

Onsen, like all Japanese baths, are exclusively for relaxation, not for cleaning. So, before entering any Japanese bath you are expected to wash and rinse your body. At an Onsen, this is part of the relaxation process and performed both thoroughly and leisurely.

The second thing I noticed was that after sweating in hot water, no one washes, on the way out. I thought this odd, considering the Japanese obsession with cleanliness.

DRIVING:
• As in North America, a green light in Japan is green. However, they call it "blue."

• Cars and streets are about one-third smaller than in North America. Therefore, city maps look more crowded.

• The streets are so narrow and tight that there are a lot of blind corners, so you'll notice a lot of mirrors mounted at corners... it's the only way to know if someone is about to enter the intersection.

• Drivers always back into parking spots.

• There are virtually no street signs or house numbers in my in-laws' town. I still have no idea how the mail gets delivered... or a pizza, for that matter. I have read that big cities work on a grid system and that delivering mail involves a lot of training.

• In an emergency, you dial 1-1-9 instead of 9-1-1.

LANGUAGE:

• Perhaps the most obvious thing is that the language is a barrier. What surprised me, and may surprise you, is just how high that barrier is. Not only will you not be able to understand or participate in conversations, but you will be unable to read so that, sometimes, just choosing the right bathroom will be a challenge. This reduces you to the dependency level of a four-year-old

• There is no "L" section in a Japanese-English dictionary.

THE PEOPLE:

• In Canada, my five foot nine inches (175 cm) is about average and a lot of men are taller than me, so, the first time I visited Japan, I looked forward to being the tallest one in a crowd and imagined myself being able to see over the all the heads. But, in the very first entirely Japanese crowd I encountered in Tokyo, all of the younger men were at least as tall as me, and most were taller. I did tower over the average woman, though. Turns out, that due to dietary improvements, the younger generations tend to be taller. The average height in Japan is currently

Something familiar but with unfamiliar flavor: Apple Pie Kit Kat (left) and Matcha Tea Kit Kat (right). It's also worth noting that most potato chips on store shelves are not salt flavour, but sushi or nori (sea weed).

five foot eight inches (178 cm) and increasing, each year.

• As well as increasing their height, a more modern diet, which now includes frozen and fast foods, has resulted in a visible number of overweight people. I have noticed the difference over the fifteen years I've been traveling to Japan. Based on observations made during my last trip, I'd say that about 20% of the people are above their ideal weight.

• Japanese women admire pale-skinned, Western beauty. They try to stay out of the sun to keep their skin youthful, and rely on long gloves, umbrellas or even skin whiteners to emulate the Western look. Their efforts to adhere to this ideal prevent them from being outdoorsy.

• Public displays of affection are frowned upon. Younger people are demonstrative enough to hold hands, but older people—including

Inago (locust) is a common snack food in many areas. I tried it. It actually tasted good, but I hated picking bug feet out from between my teeth.

An Asian girl's fingernail. Also, novelty imitations of family seals. This one represents Yokokawa, my wife's family-name. Official versions of these stamps, called inkan, are still used in Japan to verify identity on important documents.

my wife, while we're in Japan—would be embarrassed by this. I never saw any other form of touching in public.

• Japanese will praise you highly for the least achievement. Do not let it go to your head. They don't mean it. They are measuring your humility. They like humility.

• The Japanese are masters of understatement and self-deprecation. If a Japanese person says that they have taken a Karate lesson, you may expect that they are, in fact, a first-degree black belt. They are constantly amused by foreigners who exaggerate their abilities. So, unless you are fluent, I would not mention that you know a couple of Japanese words. If you always understate your abilities, you will be well received.

• If you are a foreigner, you are exempt from almost every rule: That you behave strangely is a given. However they will appreciate any attempt to learn their language and accommodate to their customs.

Though years ahead of us in cell phone use and tech, they still have a lot of phone booths. But, interestingly, though so many people are glued to their screens while on buses, trains and stations, they never talk on them in public venues. Aboard a train it's often crowded, yet eerily quiet.

The Japanese Giant Hornet; a 3-inch-long wasp! When my father encountered one, his only comment was, "I want to go home!" It is the only logical response.

• When a toddler loses a tooth they throw it on top or under the house: Lower tooth on the roof so it grows a healthy replacement, straight down and upper teeth under the house so it grows a healthy replacement, upwards. Go figure. Not sure what they do when Grandpa loses his teeth.

• The Japanese are profoundly practical. When faced with a religious decision between Shinto and Buddhism, they generally choose both. Japanese homes often have two separate shrines. Perhaps frustrating to religions everywhere, the Japanese see no hypocrisy in selecting bits and pieces that they like from each religion. This may be the wisest thing I have ever heard.

The Japanese borrow only those elements from a religion that they feel are valuable. As a result, they assimilate and accommodate many religions, without conflict. In most homes I've visited, you would see both Shinto (above left, and inset) as well as Buddhist (right) elements, like these two shrines in my father-in-law's home.

Manhole covers in Japanese cities are much more decorative than in Canada.

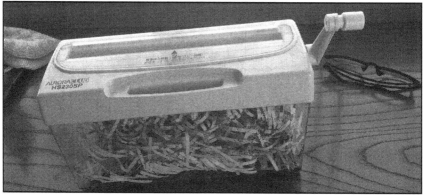

A hand-cranked document shredder. Don't know if this is a Japanese thing, but I've never come across one anywhere else.

Door to door milk delivery is still available.

JANGLISH: Examples of weird English is a many. Especially prevalent, are strange-English T-shirts for toddlers and teens. I think they try to be edgy but often end up inappropriately sexual. One toddler's shirt I saw, read: "Call me, bitch!"

I wish I'd brought one from Canada that was labeled "Larry" or "Lilith" which I could slip onto the store shelf, to enhance someone's day.

Ten Days and Five Canadians in Japan, eh.

In April of 2015, I took my parents on a ten-day tour of the Japan that I have come to know. What follows is a chronicle of that journey.

As is often the case with intricately detailed arrangements, things did not go entirely as planned. It did not turn out to be the exotic and restful vacation that I had promised them.

On the other hand, they survived.

And, let's face it, if you haven't learned that *"if something sounds too good to be true, then it probably is"* by the time you're 75, then you probably deserve what you get.

CHAPTER 9

A Writer's Mind
(It's a jungle in there!)

Tonight, I sat down to write an article on human behavior and how we all advertise to each other in subtle ways. But then I started thinking about how I started thinking about that topic, and how much I live in my own mind.

This led to memories of a bad breakup in which my own mind kind of turned on me. From here I remembered Rose, a customer of mine who I wanted to ask out but didn't, and how broken my mind and soul were at the time, and how it was probably best I didn't ask; and, anyway, I think there was a distinct possibility that she would have said no.

I was about 40 at the time, and eventually, all the psychic turmoil made me realize that certain aspects of my character needed an overhaul and that it was past time that I started "giving back" to society. So I began donating blood and sponsored an African child, through World Vision. Since then, I have saved countless lives with my 60-plus pints of AB Negative, and now sponsor two children and also help improve life for 18 poor families in the Philippines. There are statues of me in the park in my mind, but there's also a lot of pigeon poop. Mostly, cats hang out there. I'm not a big fan of cats.

That dark period also made me realize that living entirely within my own brain was not balanced and that I needed a way to shut off my mind, from time to time. I started going to the gym. A couple of regulars have commented how hard I work at the exercises and each time I thought, "That's so true. You'd think I'd be in better shape. If I had worked this hard when I was 30, I'd look like The Terminator but instead, because I'm 56, I look like Arnold Schwarzenegger... twenty years from now." But I can't say all of that because I'm too busy gasping for air, so I simply grimace and say, "I just know how to make it look hard." The sheer battle to overcome my natural sedentary tendencies followed by throbbing bones, torn ligaments and aching muscles did prove to be the distraction I'd hoped for; as did the smell of A535.

Then I had children and suddenly no longer had to worry about hitching too long a ride on any train of thought. Best I can do these days is one zone, then the train gets rerouted to a siding by "Dad, how long are you going to be? I need to poo," or "Dad, are you being a writer right now, or just watching TV?" or "Look Dad. Look. Lookit. Lookit!"

Having thought all of these thoughts, I wanted to take down some notes but I was in the bath and didn't have my smartphone, but knew that I probably wouldn't have used it anyway as I prefer paper and pen. From here I started thinking about how I don't text while I drive because that would be dangerous, but instead when brilliance strikes, I scramble for a pen while steering with one hand, one eye on the road. Then I thought about how the clipboard suction-cupped to my dash had broken which means that I have to scramble for paper now, too, and will have to drive with the steering wheel between my teeth, while being brilliant. It's almost inevitable that someday, my kids will be able to exclaim, "There's Daddy's car, again, on YouTube!"

Broken things reminded me that we are only three weeks away from leaving for Japan to see my wife's family and I have so much left to do before I go. I'm taking my parents with us on this trip and I thought of the hilarity that will ensue when my father is faced with such things as raw egg on noodles—or, in fact, even just noodles. He's always said he'd never travel to any country that didn't have a Domino's Pizza! Of all the pizza in the world, why Domino's? No idea. Why a benevolent, bearded white man looking down from the clouds? Apparently, it really doesn't take much to start the ideology ball rolling.

To be fair, Dad credits Domino's Pizza with saving his life in Mexico—while staying in an all-inclusive resort with my sister...

DAD *(grumbling)*: Nothing tastes the same here.

SISTER: Are you saying that all of this Mexican food tastes foreign? Strange that.

DAD: Something's off.

SISTER *(exasperated sigh)*: Dad, it's a Mars bar.

DAD: A sign.

SISTER: Of what? Senility?

DAD: Over there. That sign... Domino's Pizza. Finally, something Canadian!

SISTER: Their head office is in Michigan. When did Michigan become a province?

DAD: About the same time that Nacho chips became supper.

You wouldn't think so, but Dad's a survivor. He'll probably stuff his pockets with M&M's at the airport and actually gain weight in Japan. And, perhaps, start a new religion.

Anyway, I looked it up and Japan does have Domino's Pizza. It's a bit of a shame, really, as I could possibly get on board an M&M-based religion but it would depend on the core philosophy: peanut or chocolate. I could not worship a peanut God. That would be ridiculous.

This all led to how much my father will enjoy it when my Japanese father-in-law takes him gambling. Though they have no common language they actually get on very well which sometimes makes me wish that my wife and I didn't share a common language. (She often claims we don't. At least, I think that's what she's saying.)

Neither man can understand the other but they especially seem to enjoy gambling together although it almost certainly means that one of them has no clue how to play the games. I guess it's fortunate that losing can be competently achieved without knowledge.

That made me realize that there is no way that I will be able to interpret gambling lingo between my father and father-in-law.

Then I remembered my own two gambling experiences in Japan and I chuckled.

So now I'm writing about gambling in Japan.

Such is the muddled mind of a writer.

Sorry you had to see that.

CHAPTER 10

T-Minus Five Days

Day -5: Wednesday, April 8, 2015:

It's five days before we're to leave on a month-long trip to Japan. We're taking my parents with us and it's been in the works for more than two years

I stop in at my parent's house to discuss details and, as soon as I open the door, I am assaulted by the acrid smell of Vick's VapoRub. It's two o'clock in the afternoon and my mother is still in bed. She's in the throes of a full-on bronchitis attack and is trying to medicate, steam and sleep her way back to health. Meanwhile, Dad's wandering around the house in his pajamas poking through cupboards for some form of sustenance while repeating his new mantra, "I have no idea why I'm going to Japan," to which I resist replying, "Because Mom won't go without you." It might be funny, but it's completely untrue. Which is kind of funny, too.

I return home to find my 7-year-old daughter, Rihana, feverish, listless and with red rimmed eyes. Overnight, she's blossomed into a perpetual snot factory.

Meanwhile, my 10-year-old son, Noah, has become obsessed with recent air crash news and keeps asking me what it will feel like to die at various points in the journey: Hitting another plane on takeoff, Tumbling into the Pacific, Slamming into a mountain, Crashing into an apartment building. "I have absolutely no idea," I reply, each time. But, the fact that my answer never varies does not deter him. I think of mentioning that flying is safer than driving, but it seems obvious where that will lead and I don't have the patience to deal with all his queries about how it will feel to die in a parkade, by hitting a mac truck, driving off a cliff or in a McDonald's drive-thru.

My wife, Junko, is losing sleep, weight, fingernails—and some hair, I noticed, while dismantling the bathroom sink drain—because she's the one who made all of the travel arrangements and she's mortified that she might have missed some critical detail.

I check the weather in Tokyo which, this time of year, is usually 20-plus degrees Celsius, hot and sunny. Three days ago it was like that. Yesterday, it snowed for the first time in 90 years. Also, category-5 typhoon Phanfone is due to arrive tonight.

All the elements are in place and everything is going according to plan. Not my plan, however.

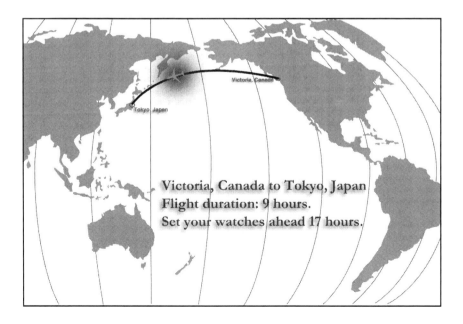

Victoria, Canada to Tokyo, Japan
Flight duration: 9 hours.
Set your watches ahead 17 hours.

CHAPTER 11

Into The East

Day 1: Mon, April 13/14

Dad's been threatening to bring along his winter jacket since we first started planning the trip. Mom says he takes it everywhere, like a security blanket. He took it to Italy in June and Vegas in August. Carried it everywhere they went. Never wore it. For close to two years, we've been telling him that Tokyo's going to be a balmy 24 degrees and the coat will be a burden. I just checked and whatever's balmy, it's not the weather. It's 14 degrees, windy and raining. I hate it when he's right.

The kids are mostly better: Rihana has only remnants of her illness; a constant but light cough like the continual sputter of a small engine—just enough to annoy all the other passengers without alerting the W.H.O. Noah feels ok but is wracked with nerves. An hour into the flight, he throws up. Then an hour after that, slightly missing the bag because he wouldn't take his eyes off the tv screen. Neighboring passengers shoved their earbuds deeper.

My acrophobic mother's antibiotics have kicked in and she's now comfortable and nose-deep into a thick book, apparently aware that we are flying in a jumbo jet toward Asia, while simultaneously oblivious to the fact that we are 40,000 feet above the Aleutians. Dad's attitude seems to be relatively good for a grumpy old man. The plane's entertainment system has poker.

Junko didn't sleep last night over worries about all the arrangements she's made but, so far, everything has gone smoothly, with the exception of the fact that she didn't sleep at all last night and is now a shell of a human being and, incidentally, our only guide and lifeline, once we touch down. Fortunately, my parents have done some studying in the two years since we first planned this trip and have almost completely memorized the word "konnichiwa" (hello), so I know that they will be ok, if we get separated.

As I carefully close the newest barf bag, I smile. For the first time in years, we didn't have to go back home to check whether Junko left her hair curler plugged in because we took it with us. Sometimes, it's the little things in life that make all the difference. As well, no one's crawling across my lap or crying in my ear, and pretty much all of the puke went into the bags. So, it's the smoothest flight I've had in 10 years.

Between barf-sessions, I notice that Air Canada has really spruced up it's international flights from five years ago, when I last traveled. The seats are more comfortable with more legroom than I recall, the meals are quite edible, the windows have electronic shutters, and the onboard entertainment system is actually entertaining. Also, the plane has been painted a light blue.

I was very impressed by the entertainment system. You can check out the in-flight menu which enhances the illusion that you have some choice. You can shop for duty-free items to lug through crowded airports and bus terminals along with the too-much luggage you already have. You can learn fun facts about Air Canada and the Boeing 787, which might give you an edge over competitors on Jeopardy as well as those crowding the escape hatches in the "unlikely event of a crash." The system even has onboard email that spams you with notifications about what the crew is doing— preparing to serve meals/drinks, preparing for landing, etc.—even though you can clearly see that they are chatting and placing side bets on the number of barf bags, or heading for the toilet with a newspaper. A detailed map displays the current GPS position of the airplane, presumably so that you can reassure yourself that you're on the right flight or to rub in the fact that you're not. In Noah's case this was especially useful for verifying that we had not yet died tragically and become the Zombie Fight from Hell. There's a travel information section, which began by relaying the impressive statistic that Japan has an almost 100% literacy rate which, apparently, you can confirm yourself by watching how may people spend time reading. According to the text, they do it everywhere, and all the time! I am pleased with myself for having brought two cameras.

As well, the system offers everything from current movies to TV shows to video games. More's the shame then that the complimentary earbuds have the audio fidelity of frayed twine tied to a rusty soup can. I watched the first five minutes of a movie then give up because the show is too good to not hear. I guess one shouldn't expect too much fun from a company that thinks a "fun fact" is that Air Canada is traded on the Toronto Stock Exchange under the symbol "AC-B.TO."

Fortunately, I have moments of brilliance and the last one was in Wal-Mart where I thought to buy earbuds for both kids. Costing only ten dollars apiece, they provide decent sound and keep the kids watching for about four of the nine hours of flying.

Junko's entertainment system is frozen. This is no fault of the airline. Rather, it's the effect she generally has on computer equipment. Fortunately the flight is not crowded and I encourage her to move to another seat with a functioning system, and a bit further from the electronics in the cockpit.

As luck would have it, Dad's entertainment console also does not work properly. Here's a taste of what it's like explaining to a 78-year-old grumpy, half-deaf man that his entertainment system is not working, over the sound of twin jet engines? (75,000 pounds of thrust, each. Fun fact!)

DAD: It's not working.

ME: Dad, it's broken.

DAD: I can't get it to work.

ME: Because it's broken.

DAD: There's no sound.

ME: There's no sound.

DAD: I think it's broken.

Finally, after moving to another seat where the sound worked well…

DAD: I can't hear anything.

Thank god for closed captions.

When we land I see some relief on the faces of my parents, and Noah's, and it strikes me as kind of funny to feel relieved while stepping off of a state-of-the-art airplane onto a dormant volcano surrounded by active quake faults, regularly swept by typhoons and tsunamis, and which has recently been irradiated.

At the airport we near the bus ticket booth and are approached by a stranger who apparently owns a "Jumbo Taxi" and can shuttle all six of us to our hotel at the same price as the bus, but with the advantage that we can leave immediately instead of waiting another hour. He insists on cash and refuses to take payment in advance, though Junko offers to pay several times.

It's 14 degrees and raining. On the ride from the airport from what little we can see out the fogged windows it looks exactly like Vancouver, except with worse weather. "It looks exactly like Vancouver, except with worse weather," says my father, obviously impressed.

As we exit the bus, our driver suddenly realizes that he has made a $20 error in his calculations and apologizes profusely while simultaneously sticking to this new, higher figure. I leave it completely to Junko to resolve all disagreements with Japanese people because their culture is so overly polite, hierarchical and contextual and I didn't pack enough Tylenol to start getting headaches this early in the trip. Junko actually pays the extra, thinking that it was still a good deal for us. That's when I realize that the common belief that everything is different in Japan applies equally to my wife.

Having reached our destination (the Mitsui Garden Hotel) our travelling ends with a flourish as Noah spectacularly pukes all over his shoes, at the lobby entrance. The Canadians have arrived!

Our room is quite basic, but clean and with a nice view. As we settle in, I notice that there are no drawers, so we will have to live out of our suitcases, which pretty much takes up all the extra space in the room.

My daughter discovers an ornately decorated ceramic vessel with an electrical cord sticking out of one end. Inside is some sort of perfume so, while my wife is in the lobby confirming details, we plug it in and enjoy the pleasant aroma. When she returns, she informs us that it is not perfume, but complimentary insecticide.

I am surprised that the wifi is not free and costs $1/15 minutes, but other than that, it all seems great. After having spent about $10,000 to get us all here I am chomping at the bit to blog what's happened so far, but $4/hour is too rich for my blood.

We settle in, then wander down to the lobby and enter the first restaurant that seems to be serving something recognizable. It's a buffet. We're all hungry, but not really that hungry… except, of course, for Noah who first regurgitated the small donut he had at breakfast and then continued throwing up so long that I wouldn't have been surprised if the last few bags were filled with baby pablum.

The buffet menu is varied, but unusual for Westerners, and of course filled with exotic seafood options. I've never seen my father eat so much salad in all my life.

The buffet costs us $170 which means that Dad's lettuce leaves were about thirty US-dollars.

My largest fear at this moment: "Just getting there is half the fun!"

(upper, left) "Family Rooms" have a separate bed for each member of the family, which certainly says something about the dynamic of Japanese married couples with kids.

(upper, right) Rihana, with Barbie and Riachu all tucked in. Interestingly, she never plays with such toys at home, but filled her backpack with them for this trip. She never played with them during the trip, either. Also, pillows are about half the size of those back home and filled with dry beans, or some such thing. I find them very comfortable, but wonder how well Mom and Dad will adjust.

(lower, left) Many people think the folding of the toilet paper a nice, professional touch and find it reassuring to know that the paper roll is fresh. I, on the other hand, can't help but be reminded that the person who cleaned the toilet has touched our toilet paper.

(lower, right) Also disconcerting to me, considering the inclement weather, the presence of a shoe dryer.

CHAPTER 12

Touring Tokyo

Day 2: Wed, April 15

While my wife and I plan the day, our two children (Rihana: 8, and Noah: 10) spend their first hour of the day in the bathroom, spraying their butts and laughing hysterically.

The Japanese toilet is a technological marvel and national treasure that is rarely seen outside of the country. It is heated, has a bidet, bum-wash and, often, a blow dryer built in, almost eliminating the need for toilet paper. Of the many spectacular sights a tourist comes across, the toilet is probably the most frequently photographed and discussed. You may enter Japan thinking of kimonos, but you leave thinking about toilets. Slogans like this are probably why I can't find work in tourism.

Just before we leave, I lift the kids onto my lap and give them a briefing about today's plans, reminding them how we expect them to behave. Noah, seems to be fully recovered from yesterday's barf-fest, however I point out that he is wearing his last clean pair of pants. When they hop off my lap they leave a damp splotch.

Last night we paid five dollars for a leaf of lettuce. Consequently, this morning we dine in the lobby, on factory-baked goods and a coffee-colored liquid from the hotel's convenience store.

Our hotel is located in Chiba, a district just north of Tokyo-proper. We plan to visit Disney Sea as well as Tokyo and this is relatively convenient for both. A bus- and train-ride later, we arrive at Tokyo Station, in downtown Tokyo. It's about 9am and we're off to a good start.

Tokyo Station is about four city blocks square and several layers deep. It is the central hub for every train, subway and bullet train but also, haphazardly dispersed between platforms, are about a hundred shops that form a rabbit warren-like mall.

Even for a native, navigating Tokyo's transit system can be a trial. And if that's the trial, then navigating Tokyo Station is the part where you are arrested in a back alley and beaten by cops on the take, before being roughly escorted downtown to the station—er—even though downtown at a station is exactly where you already are. Perhaps, not the best metaphor.

Though we are surrounded by a highly sophisticated and efficient transit system, we walk about four miles, getting oriented. It takes Junko an hour to find the proper ticket booth to book our seats on the Bullet Train to Kyoto where we plan to be, in a couple of days. While she does this, the rest of us circle up the wagons into a small cluster, and stand safely huddled out of the way of Tokyo business people hurrying by, apparently all late for the same appointment. The sheer number of people is so staggering that individuals become meaningless, like bubbles in foam.

In Japan, public spaces like train stations and malls offer limited seating. In Tokyo, this probably has to do with the high cost of real estate. If you want to sit, you're going to have to buy something. Mom is not used to being on her feet so long and asks if we can find a coffee shop where she can sit for a few minutes. Truthfully, we all feel the same way. We wander for another hour in search of a place serving something resembling coffee and a doughnut, and come up empty. Meanwhile, Dad, who is attacking Japan as if he considers himself on an episode of Survivor-Dad, spots McDonald's and veers off to enjoy an early lunch. Thus my parents get their first taste of McJapanese cuisine.

It is well known that for a long time, Japan was an insular nation. Recently, the Japanese have been making an effort to embrace the outside world by doing things like encouraging tourism and hosting the 2020 Olympics. But one obstacle is their long cultural tradition of cash-only transactions. Fifteen years ago, on my first trip to Japan, credit cards were not accepted anywhere. Modern Japan now accepts credit cards at about two thirds of the places you might go, but the exceptions can be unexpected. One place that is still not equipped to accept them is the McDonald's, in Tokyo Station.

Also unexpected was that McDonald's did not have individually portioned salt packets. When my Father casually asked for salt, he caused a small panic at the cash register followed by what I can't resist referring to as a mcflurry of activity in the kitchen. What he ended up getting was a small fries bag, half filled with enough salt to melt ten thousand slugs.

In the bathroom, my Mother notices a baby seat fastened to the wall so that mothers can safely stow their fussy bundles of joy, while relieving themselves. This is a clever Japanese convenience that has not been installed in the men's room, thus reflecting typical Japanese family culture.

While attempting to find the correct exit, our expedition comes across a Pokemon shop that is, appropriately, about the size of a Pokeball. For Noah, this is equivalent to discovering the Ark of the Covenant. As we enter, he loudly declares that he is so filled with joy that he feels like crying. When he sees Pokemon socks, he begins jumping up and down and babbling in tongues. I know that such demonstrative joy is because Noah is home schooled and unspoiled, but to the outside world, he probably appears simple.

Excerpt from Survivor-Dad Japan, Personal Journal: "Hans has gone mad and Fritz is chewing his fingers to stubs. I, alone, have managed to survive, though it has not been without compromise. I can no longer remember the face of my waitress at the Monkey Tree Pub, or the last time I smiled. How much longer I can hold on, is uncertain. This may be my final entry."

Noah's tenth birthday is a couple of days away and his grandparents seize the opportunity to shower him with gifts instilling in him the idea that although Mom and Dad might love him more, Grammy and Grampy love him better. As well, I believe, they hope to raise his already excessive expectations so that living with him becomes as impossible for Junko and I as living with me was for them, thus completing the karmic cycle.

They buy him a small plush "Dedenne," a mug and the socks, all of which he deems so valuable that he makes us wait ten minutes while he stows them securely in his backpack so that he can properly preserve the shopping bag they came in which sports a large picture of Pikachu. He folds that neatly and makes me promise to keep it safe and, somehow, unwrinkled in my backpack. Why he has no room for a folded plastic bag the thickness of three human hairs, I have no idea. My son might just be a bit obsessive but we dare not mention it because we're not sure that he could handle the fact that the letters OCD are not in alphabetical order.

Noah spends the rest of the day grinning ear to ear, hugging the stuffy and thanking Grammy and Grampy as profusely as if accepting an Academy Award.

It's almost noon by the time we find our way to the surface world.

The spectacular Asakusa gate and temple is probably the most visited shrine in all of Japan by virtue of being pretty much next door to Tokyo Station. On this day, every tourist in Japan has decided to visit there. The sky is cloud-scudded and the weather oscillates from gusty and cold to sunny and blazing hot. Consequently, my backpack is swollen with coats and sweaters that are rarely used, and as I navigate the thick sea of tourists, I feel like a pregnant bull *(note to self: change this simile before anyone sees it)* while at the same time come to understand why mules are so ornery.

Dad offers to take my video camera and get some footage of me. This will be the first time I have appeared in our family videos and the fact that Junko is not a single mother of two may provide as big a surprise to viewers as the big twist in the movie The Crying Game.

No one can enjoy Jeopardy, Wheel of Fortune, a crossword or Suduko with my mother in the room. She reads a lot and knows things that she has no right in knowing. As we walk through the huge gate and human bumper-car our way down the narrow lane, toward the main temple, I call upon my years of experience in things Japanese and try to play tour guide. It's a short play that ends abruptly.

ME: ...and these are tourists, and those are flowers. Over there is some sort of temple, probably Japanese. The stuff in this shop is just cheap Chinese crap.

MOM: Actually, I think those might be reproductions of Netsuke...

ME: Netsu-what now?

MOM: Netsuke. Intricately carved buttons attached to the sashes of robes and used to secure pouches and purses, because traditional-style Japanese robes have no pockets.

I am nonplussed, but cover with my best plussed look.
ME: Well, of course. I meant cheap Chinese *imitations.*

Tourists throng the thousand shops that line the lane leading to the Buddhist temple at Asakusa.

MOM: Are you sure, Honey? To me, those look to be faithful, hand made reproductions; Edo period, judging by the design. And I'm pretty sure that they're real ivory. You can't always tell Ivory from bone without weighing it or using a magnifying glass, but these have the appropriate luster and smoothness as well as the distinctive tawny patina from absorbing oils from people who have handled them.

ME: How do you know all of that?

MOM: Oh. I'm not sure. Probably read it in a novel, or something.

ME: Hmpf! Novels.

I want to appear unflappable, so to disguise the fact that I am flapped, I quickly turn away and pretend to scan the milling throng. My backpack takes down a Chinese tour group and a small child licking an ice cream cone.

ME: Every tourist shop in Tokyo must be crowded onto this one street.

MOM: If I'm not mistaken, in the old days, going to temple was an important religious and social event. Streets leading to temples were very busy so that is where shop keepers preferred to set up shop. I think this must be a modern reflection of that.

ME: Oh look. Ice cream!

In front of the temple is a large urn of sand from which sticks of incense glow and smoke. Before entering the temple, people waft the sacred smoke over ailing parts of their body, with prayers of healing. My mother, who is still recovering from her Bronchitis does a cursory wave which imperceptibly disturbs a single wispy tendril. Later, she points out a Chinese tourist wafting and inhaling smoke, an unlit cigarette dangling from his lips.

I have a short list in my head of things I want to do with my parents, beyond sightseeing: 1) Have a beer with my father in a traditional Japanese bar (izakaya), 2) take them to a traditional Japanese bath (onsen), 3) get them to try Japanese food, preferably sushi, and 4) get a picture of them with a girl in a kimono. When I spot a couple of Asian girls in decorative kimonos surrounded by selfie-snapping tourists I quickly send Junko to ask them if they would pose with my parents for a picture. They agree and I am pleased to get the money shot. As we walk away, Junko tells me that they were not Japanese, but tourists who rented the costume for the day and got caught in the ultimate tourist trap, unable to extricate themselves from a never ending photo-op. In Tokyo, I guess, real Japanese women wearing real kimonos must be perpetually late for appointments.

Inside the temple, we do the typical tourist-thing and follow the crowd, posing and snapping pictures. Everything is intensely detailed and our senses are quickly overwhelmed. We come away understanding little more than that it is all very Japanese-y.

Dad is convinced that of all the food in Japan, he will only be able to handle tempura. Luck is with us and we quickly find a "Tempura Hut"—or, at least, the Japanese equivalent. But somehow,

The spectacular main gate, at Asakusa.

we have managed to find the only Japanese restaurant in the world that does not have soy sauce on the table. Strangely, Dad notices and surprises us all by demanding some. The restaurateurs are proud of their homemade tempura sauce and I sense that ordering soy is akin to asking a Michelin-starred chef for ketchup. But they comply. He then further surprises us by ordering green tea. I have never seen him drink tea of any color. When it arrives, he practically empties the container of soy into his tea. Caucasian and Asians alike are startled and, no doubt, grossed out.

As they clear the dishes, the waitress asks my Father how he liked the meal, though the fact that they have only eaten about four small bites seems an obvious indicator. As I strike #3 off my wish list, Dad replies that it was not crispy and makes odd gestures with his fingertips, as if massaging a cob of corn, to which she nods, smiles and quickly disappears. I can only hope there is a dictionary in the kitchen. This particular style of tempura is not crispy because the final stage of preparation is to douse it in the restaurant's original tempura sauce, for which it is famous. Dad declares that there is now nothing in the country he can eat, except, of course McDonald's or Domino's Pizza.

Japanese restaurants do not normally provide napkins because most Japanese carry a handkerchief, so my Father leaves the restaurant a celebrity, with a soy sauce mustache.

We take a guided tour on a ferry filled to capacity with European and Chinese tourists. The tour guide welcomes everyone in English and then, as we float around Tokyo Bay she gives an hour-long narration on everything to the left and right, entirely in Japanese. From this I learn the Japanese words for left and right.

During the ferry ride, I notice that Noah is looking a bit peaked. Thinking ahead, Dad and I search our possessions for an impromptu sick bag and can find only one, Noah's prized Pokemon bag. Dad and I exchange glances and I ready the video camera. I am both glad and disappointed that The Moment never comes.

The ferry takes us to Odaiba, an artificial island with a fantastic view of Tokyo's Rainbow Bridge and which is home to the distinctive Fuji TV building and the Diver City Tokyo Plaza, a broad walkway linking several malls and decorated by impressive statues (including a 36-foot (11m) tall reproduction of the Statue of Liberty) and other works of art. Among them is a full-scale (60ft/18m tall) model of Gundam, a famous anime robot. We've heard that the statue moves, at regularly scheduled intervals; the next show 30 minutes away. The winds have picked up to almost gale-force, sweeping the heat of the day, and my body, inland. We decide to wait for the big show, huddled behind one of Gundam's gigantic legs that acts as a satisfactory wind break. Just so that you know, this is one of those rare instances in which hiding behind a 60-foot giant that is breaking wind, is a good idea. Finally, lights begin to flash over Gundam's body and his head moves from side to side. Heart pounding music builds to a dramatic crescendo and a deep and commanding voice yells, *"Gundam, iki masu!"* (Gundam, go!) at which point, Gundam dramatically tilts his head subtly skyward. "Who, me?" he seems to be asking. It's so spectacular that it's difficult to ascertain exactly when the show ends; people simply drift away. Junko thinks that it would be a great joke if, at the very end,

(left) Ironically, we have never been more not in New York. Surprisingly, there are at least two other Statue of Liberty reproductions, elsewhere in Japan. (right) Still-pictures more than adequately capture the excitement of the Gundam "action" extravaganza.

Gundam waved goodbye. But he doesn't.

On our way home, an interesting interaction occurs between my wife and another Japanese woman. We all follow a small maze of roped off alleyways to get in line behind a couple of other families. Five minutes later, another family, led by the mother, files through from the opposite side and ends up shoulder to shoulder with us, though there is now a lineup behind us. We then realize that there are two lanes marked with the same signage; two paths to the same bus. On the surface, Junko appears unfazed, but my spider senses are tingling. She's definitely angry at the woman who she feels has butted in. I can tell that the other woman is equally disgruntled when Junko makes the first move, and we board before her. Both feel that the other one has violated proper Japanese protocol. Both are right and no one is wrong, but both are mad. To give you some context: The bus can hold about 70 people. In all, there are 14 in the line. It all has the familiar feel of marriage.

By the end of the day, we've thoroughly tested Tokyo asphalt as well as the transit system, having taken a bus, subway, monorail, several trains, two ferries and walked for miles, in between. Mom, Dad and the kids have also been tested, I think.

After a reasonably priced and Western-style dinner at the hotel, we say goodnight to Mom and Dad as they return to their room to apply A535.

We head to the Hotel's rooftop Onsen (traditional Japanese bath) to relax. These are, basically, large hot tubs where people bathe naked, communally. Because everyone is naked, men and women bathe in separate facilities. Noah and I spend a relaxing half hour being gawked at by Japanese children.

I noticed two strange things, this time, that I had never noticed before. The first thing was that, in the change room, the other men tended to cover their naughty bits with a small towel, even though we are all male, and all soon to be exposed.

Onsen, like all Japanese baths, are exclusively for relaxation, not for cleaning. So, before entering any Japanese bath you are expected to wash and rinse your body. At an Onsen, this is part of the relaxation process and performed both thoroughly and leisurely.

The second thing I noticed was that after sweating in hot water, no one washes on the way out, which I thought odd, considering how obsessed the Japanese are with cleanliness.

I have no insights into either behavior other than the obvious—that we are still in Japan.

CHAPTER 13

Disney Sea

Day 3: Thu, April 16th

It's a big day for me. Like most every parent I know, I've drummed my fingers through all those boring, early years, waiting only for the time when I could introduce my children to the wonders of Disneyland and vicariously revel in their open-mouthed awe, while dabbing the corners of their mouths with a tissue.

It's also a big day for my ten-year-old son, Noah: He gets to wear his new Pokemon socks. For him, the prospect of going to Disneyland pales in comparison.

I really hate that little guy's shirt.

As all of the adults in our group have been to Disneyland, we opted to visit Disney Sea, an alternate Disney theme park, exclusive to Japan. Based on a YouTube video he saw of girls singing and dancing in the opening show, Noah has bet me $10 that he will not enjoy Disney Sea. He has no interest in singing, dancing or girls. It's not so much that he is pre-adolescent, but more that none of those things are Pokemon-related. In a few years, he will probably change his mind about girls. And, I am confident that within hours he will change his mind about Disney Sea. Then, I will be able to see my children smiling in reverential wonder at how pleasurable an idealized replica of life can be. Also, I will be ten dollars richer—though $300 poorer. I would pay double if I could change his obsessed mind about Pokemon, but there are limits to what even Disney can accomplish.

Turns out, I owe Noah ten dollars!

I'm sure this shocks you as much as it did me, but Disney Sea is not for everyone, and this time, it was not for us.

The day we went, the weather was fantastic and the crowds were relatively light. All conditions seemed optimal. We entered through the South gate and strolled through the inner courtyard (a kind of holding area) before the main gates open. The courtyard was beautiful enough to keep us gawking throughout the 30-minute wait.

The Venetian Gondola ride was cool, but not as cool as I thought, having almost nothing to do with Venus.

The main gates opened and we leisurely found a cafe to sit and have a morning coffee and pastry. We spent the first hour admiring the coffee and pastry. The setting was also nice. Afterward, we watched the opening show, which took place directly in front of the cafe.

"And now, for your entertainment, our own Disney Sea Performers present Disney Sea's Fashion Fantasmic...." were the last words we heard in English. In Disneyland, everything is labeled in English, as well as Japanese, but almost all dialogue is entirely in Japanese. The spectacular opening performance involved singing, dancing and amazing costumes which helped spin a tale involving the four seasons and fashion, I think.

What I did not realize is that, beyond being a truly magical kingdom, Disney in Japan is also an exam for which you are expected to study. Remembering my experience in America's Disneyland, 30 years previous, I chose a very laid-back approach. If you only have one day there, this is a mistake. The crowds were lighter back then, and also, they were less Asian. Having done some research, after the fact, I have learned that Japanese crowds are keeners who arrive at the gates 1-2 hours before opening, armed with a strategy, bottled water and running shoes for the sprint to the most popular attraction.

For people teenaged and beyond, I have no reservations in recommending Disney Sea. The level of detail in the magical facades is staggering. For the entire eight hours we were there, I walked around like a wide-eyed zombie muttering, "Wow. Wow. Wow. Wow." until my jaw ached and my neck seized. Adults will enjoy strolling, dining and snapping pictures. Teenagers, for whom time is less valued, can run from ride to ride and spend 90 minutes in line gabbing with their friends before experiencing the most thrilling 90 seconds of their lives.

For younger kids, the long waits for the best rides can be a problem. My kids are amazingly patient, having spent half their lives in my wife's shopping cart, but I felt sad that they might only be able to get to a couple of the best rides. In the end, we managed one popular ride and about five of the less popular ones. But this was mostly due to our lack of preparation and our poor attitude toward stressing while on vacation.

My Disney Sea Pro Tips:

1) The Fastpass System: Before you go, you should thoroughly understand the Fastpass system now used to reduce wait-times. Purchase your tickets in advance, and make sure that you buy a Fastpass. (On peak days, there is a limit to the number issued.) You can only use your Fastpass for one ride at a time but it allows you to make a reservation to bypass the regular line and join the priority-boarding lineup. Without a Fastpass, wait times in the ordinary lines can exceed 90 minutes. (Fun Fact: Disney Sea is the world record holder for the longest theme park wait time of 500 minutes for Toy Story Mania, when it was new, in 2012!) We found 60 minutes to be the norm for any of the popular rides. The Fastpass gives you a window of time during which you can freely enter the priority lineup. In this line, you will only have to wait about 20 minutes. But, as you can only reserve one ride at a time, this means that if your first reservation is late in the day, your pass is almost useless. If you wait, like we did, before going to your favorite ride and employing your Fastpass, your reservation time will likely end up being after dark. If so, do not use the Fastpass, proceed to your second-favorite ride and use it there. Otherwise, the Fastpass will be tied up for most of the day. So, get to your must-do ride immediately after the gates open.

View from DaVinci castle.

Then head for your second favorite and check out the line. If it's too long, proceed to the next priority or just wander and have ice cream.

2) Check the calendar. Avoid holidays and go early in the week (Monday to Thursday).

3) How Long To Stay: I'd say that it would take three days to thoroughly explore the park, without rushing. But if you plan well, a lot can be done in one, though it's impossible to try every ride in a single day.

4) Plan ahead and get there on time. Memorize the layout and main attractions that interest you. Also check websites to find out which attractions are currently the most popular. Some of these sites are surprisingly accurate in estimating wait times. Plan your day in advance. Unlike in America, Japanese visitors arrive 1-2 hours prior to gate opening, and they have all done their homework, have memorized a strategy and immediately race to their favorite rides. They use their Fastpasses strategically and, an hour after opening, yours will be rendered useless because of all the reservations ahead of you.

5) If you're determined to ride as many rides as possible, count on spending the majority of your day in lineups. It's really best to go it alone, or in couples, because that size of group can move relatively quickly and be most flexible. If a large group has to agree, there will be a lot of compromise and the time wasted in negotiating can eat into the number of rides you can get to. At the age of 56, I no longer see the balance in one minute of boredom for every one second of adventure, but then I'm a writer and I'm always thinking, "I could be home writing something amazing." Which, of course, presupposes that I am capable of writing something amazing, and also that there is nothing on TV. Nothing!

6) Not everyone wants to ride. Local business people often come after work to spend a leisurely evening in this magical Mediterranean fantasyland. If you are happy to just wander, stand only in lines that seem conveniently short, snap pictures and eat in the seven exotic settings, then you can easily justify the cost. If so, and if you have a Fastpass, remember to give it to another of your party so that they can reserve extra rides.

7) Small children: This system is not great for those with small children. Our kids are exceptional at waiting, but I felt bad for them after waiting for more than an hour for a 90-second roller coaster ride. In truth, I may have been more frustrated than they were. They weren't thrilled to have to bypass all the coolest rides, but three days later, via Skype, they talked to their friends about it in glowing terms.

The Unexpected:
• In preparation for one of the street events, attendants cleared a large space in one of the town squares. It was soon lined by experienced patrons who obviously knew what was coming and where best to sit. For more than 30 minutes people walked around the clearing instead of taking the shortcut, straight through. It was all exceptionally orderly. This degree of respect for low-level authority does not exist in my country. Canadian moms with strollers would be leaping over the thin line of seated onlookers, cutting across continually. In Texas, there would be gun play.

• The Japanese are making an earnest effort but still do not understand all the elements required to provide a truly welcoming environment for foreigners. Even at Disney Sea, most of the employees do not speak more than a smattering of English. Coupled with my smattering of Japanese, I was readily able to find a toilet, but getting restaurant or ride information had to be left to Junko. I've read that there is always an English-speaking attendant close by, and you will be guided to one if map-pointing and pantomime fail to do the trick.

• All employees at all Disneylands are skilled in the art of maintaining a wide, fake grin for the duration of their shift. The Japanese, who have a reputation for grasping a new concept and improving upon it, have the largest and fakest of all the smiles.

• It was also interesting to me the ways in which the intensely-attentive Japanese can fail to be helpful. They are always ultra-polite and you feel as if they are trying their hardest to solve your problem, but while their smiles wrap around to the back of the heads I sometimes wondered why they created the problem in the first place. Other times they offer help, but not to any extent that is actually useful...

Case Study #1: A group of five ignorant Canadians enter through the South Gate and are handed a site map/guide, which has the front page in English and the interior entirely in Japanese. Eventually, they deduce that, because it's Disneyland, there must be English instructions somewhere. They look but cannot find, and finally decide to ask the attendant who has been silently watching and smiling like The Joker for the last 10 minutes. She deftly extracts a fully English version of the pamphlet from a hidden cabinet. As helpful as she was, one can't help wondering why the English version wasn't offered, at the outset. (Bonus Pro Tip: reams of unread Japanese Disney Sea pamphlets can be found in the trashcan, five feet from the entrance.)

Case Study #2: A group of five ignorant Canadians who entered via the South gate accidentally exit via the North gate. They are confused that the bus stops and car park seem to be the exact mirror of the ones they remember. Eventually, they realize that they are lost and return to the gate to ask for help. The attendant could simply let them back in (it's closing time) and allow them to walk about 30 feet and exit through the South gate into familiar territory, but instead, he very politely and patiently instructs them on how to find their way around the building. Not the easiest solution, but, I suspect, the solution he thought we—er, I mean "they"—deserved.

* * *

This is our final day at this hotel, which has a spectacular free onsen on the top floor. Onsens are communal soaking tubs based on hot and cold springs of earlier times. Because the bathing is done naked, the genders have separate facilities. I try to convince my parents to unwind the Japanese way with a naked soak, but my mother says she's not getting naked in front of a bunch of beautiful Japanese girls, and my father sees no point in getting naked without them.

So much for number two, on my must-do list.

If you are refering to the map at Disney Sea, you've got a problem because everyone else knows exactly where they are going and are rushing to take your spot on the best rides.

CHAPTER 14

Modern Tokyo to Historic Kyoto

Day 4: Fri, April 17th

The modern Bullet Train *(Shinkansen)* is more like an airplane than a train and includes stewardesses offering snacks and beverages. On straight stretches, the train runs at about 200 miles per hour (320 km/hr.). When passing another Shinkansen going in the opposite direction, all you see is a long white streak, its windows nothing more than a grey blur. The ride is so smooth that it's an unexpectedly unremarkable experience to travel this way. Farms and mountains in the distance give no hint of the speed. It's only when you try to glimpse scenery very close to the tracks that you realize how fast you are going. The first time I traveled to Kyoto, I spent the entire journey trying to get a picture of some of the remote villages that I glimpsed through brief breaks in the foliage. Unfortunately, we sped by so fast that I was unable to focus the camera and snap a single picture.

After three days of trains, subways and monorails, my parents are little impressed by yet another train, regardless of the speed. For the first ten minutes they look out the window. Dad spends the rest trip glued to my laptop, playing poker or asleep, dreaming about poker. Mom reads a book.

Rihana sputter-coughs.

Noah barfs. Moments later, he proudly announces that his vomit was going more than 200 miles per hour, as it entered the bag. I point out that his current record remains untouched at 570 miles per hour (913 kph.), during the flight from Canada. We are all as impressed as we are grossed out.

I told my parents that they could look forward to seeing the iconic Mount Fuji, but clouds obscure the view and we speed by a vista of fog, instead.

Our hotel in Kyoto, ANA Crowne Plaza Kyoto, is located directly across the street from Nijo Jo (Nijo Castle), once the home of the Royal Family, when Kyoto was the capital, before 1868. The hotel is upscale from the family-oriented one we just left; has several fancy restaurants that offer a variety of cuisine and a luxurious lobby and lounge. We are greeted by beautiful young girls in kimonos and Dad uses the word "Geisha" about ten times, as they lead us to our rooms.

Left: Entrance Gate to Nijo Castle, famous for its "Nightengale Floors." Right: Looking at the floorboards, from beneath, you can see the specially designed nails meant to squeak, to expose intruders. Bottom: What Mt. Fuji looks like whenever my parents are not in Japan.

CHAPTER 15

First Taste of Kyoto

Day 5: Sat, April 18th

Our accommodation is a Kyoto highlight. Everyone is happy here. Mom and Dad have no trouble with the menu. Meanwhile, Junko and the kids have found a nearby breakfast restaurant they prefer over the hotel's. And so, the three of us—Mom, Dad and I— enjoy starting our days off with recognizable coffee and good conversation, at the breakfast buffet. I notice that a slow start, comfort food and a happy crowd at breakfast is critical to a good day.

 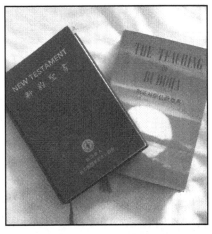

In the hotel garden: It struck me that so much loose change could never exist in a public space in Canada. Bible versus Buddha: Some hotels provide both books. The Japanese have a long tradition of melding many religions into one, personal philosophy.

Also, I am learning a lot about my parents talking to them, one on one, like this.

Junko has done a great job of organizing the trip, so far. She's been a fantastic tour guide, but thinks nothing of transferring from bus to train to subway. All the waiting and walking do not seem to wear her down the way it does the rest of us.

The kids are still not at full steam. Both suffer bouts of nausea as we travel, and sightseeing is not their favorite activity. They don't complain much, but are not enthusiastic to start another day. On the other hand, we've so lowered their expectations that when we come across a small park with a seesaw, they jump for joy and spend a happy hour teetering and tottering. A ten-year-old and eight-year-old so enthusiastically playing on a seesaw may appear mentally challenged, but you can't ignore their happiness. I think their time at Disney Sea has taught them the value of anything with a short queue.

Junko takes us to Fushimi Inari-Taisha a shrine dedicated to the god of rice. Somehow, a rice-loving fox is also involved. The most memorable feature is a 2-hour trek through a winding path under

3300 orange gates, donated by businesses, throughout Japan. Orange paint in this town is either incredibly abundant, or incredibly scarce.

We only follow the first hundred-or-so meters of the path which brings us to a series of shops and small shrines, providing at least four different ways to pray for good luck and good health, while also donating to the shrine. Religious mini-arcades like this is an idea that North American churches seriously ought to consider. One of these religious "attractions" is a wishing stone. You decide whether the stone is heavier or lighter than it looks then make a wish, before attempting to lift it. If you were correct in your guess, your wish is granted. No spoilers here, but I did not get my wish.

We stroll the crowded lanes of tourist-oriented shops and I spot some small souvenirs (omiyage) I might want, for friends back home. Junko interprets between me and the shopkeeper who delivers one of the best comeback lines I've heard in ages...

North American churches could learn a lesson in fund raising through "good luck" games, like this coin toss at The Golden Pavillion (above), and the rock lift game at the Fushimi Inari temple. (below) Noah's wishing for more Pokemon toys and I'm wishing he doesn't get them. Neither of us guessed the heft of the stone correctly, so niether of us gets our wish. Our future has never been more unclear.

ME: Maybe I should wait. I can get similar things elsewhere.

SHOPKEEPER: Yes, but you cannot get souvenirs from here, anywhere else.

I am sold. For, what is the value in a cheap, factory-made souvenir, if not purchased where it has significance?

Later in the day, Junko, the kids and I head out for some truly Japanese fare while Mom and Dad relax in the Hotel lounge with some pasta and wine. After our dinner, I join them for conversation and wine, and to enjoy the violin and guitar performance, on stage.

CHAPTER 16

The Serene Temples of Kyoto

Day 6: Sun, April 19th

During our breakfast conversations I am discovering interesting things about my parents. For instance: My mother does not have a poker face. I casually mentioned that we would soon be heading to Fukaya, Junko's hometown, and that we will all be staying at my father-in-law's house. Her face falls faster than Niagra. I remind her that Junko had debated whether to set them up in a hotel or not, and I was sure that we mentioned that either arrangement was possible. But, still, I feel bad. My mother is a quiet person who really likes her privacy. I am probably losing a dollar of my inheritance for every letter of this document.

The problem with a hotel near where Junko lives is that it would be miles away and would not have much in the way of English-speaking staff, because Fukaya is a farming area, not geared for tourists.

Another problem that recently came to light is that there are six of us and none of the family's cars that are at our disposal will carry more than four. Beyond this, Junko's license has expired. Apparently, she mentioned this to me and encouraged me to get my international driver's license, though probably not in the same sentence... or month. In dealing with Japanese—especially wives—it's always up to you to put two and two together, however far apart they might be. I did not want to drive in Japan, but if I'd known that we'd spend the entire three days of my parents' visit stranded at her rural home with no driver, I would have sucked it up.

To top it all off, the weather is still anomalous and today it's raining, over all of Japan.

This time, it's going to take more than coffee and pastry to cheer Mom up.

For the last two years, I have extolled the serenity and breath-taking beauty of The Golden Pavilion (Kinkaku-Ji), saying that if my parents see only one thing in all of Japan, this site is worth the experience.

Ten years ago, my visit to the Golden Pavilion seemed the epitome of Zen. I recall strolling the garden paths at leisure and stopping for a relaxing cup of Matcha tea, prepared and served in the traditional way by a kimono-clad woman, in a wooden hut, surrounded by forest and the sounds of birds.

Things have changed. As we near the ticket booth, three large tour buses of Chinese tourists disembark and start pushing and shoving us forward. It's lightly raining and every one of them has an umbrella, the spokes of which threaten to poke out our eyes. These Chinese are loud and a bit rude and completely disrupt my fond remembering. As we ooze along the path, pushed from behind like paste from a tube, we bask in a serenity similar to that of downtown Tokyo, at rush hour. The authentic-looking tea house where I once enjoyed the Matcha, years ago, still has a view of a serene garden, but that garden is tiny and surrounded on all sides by shops and milling tourists.

An interesting thing about Kinkaku-Ji is that, in 1950, a mad monk burned it to the ground. So, like much of the interior at Nijo Castle that we saw yesterday, what we are looking at is mostly a modern reconstruction. In the case of Kinkaku-Ji, even the gold exterior was upgraded, covering more area and made thicker and more lustrous than the original. All the world is becoming Disneyland.

At key viewing spots along the way, Dad skillfully nudges his way to the front and manages to take the same photos as a million tourists before him. The photos record a serenity that is not actually there. Who says a photo never lies?

It's ok. I have my memories and I don't like Matcha Tea, anyway. But for Mom and Dad, this is miles from what I had led them to expect. Also, it's raining.

My father is a physical anomaly. He's always been athletic, but his vigor and stamina are completely inappropriate and just plain weird for a man of his age. Of all of us, he's the one who seems to be weathering our rigorous itinerary the best.

Throughout the trip, as we negotiated stations and hopped from one transit system to another, my father has not only carried his own weight, but the weight of one of our large, jam-packed suitcases and, upon occasion, a child's jacket or cap. Many times, I've looked at him lugging all of that crap and been thankful that it allowed me the freedom to eat my donut. He may not know why he's in Japan, but I do.

I did not inherit my father's athletic prowess. My brother got that. What I got is my father's love of documenting things. My brother got that, too. The most common picture that gets taken, every time we get together for a family event, is of one or all of us taking pictures of the other(s), like some sort of Tourist standoff.

I had hoped to keep Noah amused using my still-camera to record Grammy and Grampy's trip, but he'd rather be bored than have a job. Rihana is eager but not yet skilled enough. So, I was very pleased when my father volunteered to take snapshots. I'm still documenting things with the video camera, but it's freed me up

Kinkaku-Ji, The Golden Pavillion

enough to actually see some sights and I get to be in the pictures, which is rare.

Dad's a man of action. He prefers to do things rather than just sit around the pool. He is not so enthusiastic a sightseer. But give him a camera and, suddenly, he's on a mission. He will get shots that I am too shy to take. Today, he took a picture of a rickshaw driver or engine—not sure which to call him—who I passed by because he did not seem to be in the mood. Dad captured him and his mood.

He's snapped just about every "Geisha" we've come across and yesterday, he stalked a bride and groom to document the luxurious wedding that took place at our hotel. Dad does not miss much; especially, if it's cute.

One bus ride and a sick bag later, we arrive at another Buddhist temple: Kiyomizu-dera. The main road leading to the shrine is long and steep. It's lined with shops and the crowds are thick, as we've come to expect. I am sure to hold my kids' hands tightly and keep a hawk's eye out to make sure we don't get separated. My mother is winded by the time we reach the gate of the large shrine and picturesque rambling gardens. We stop for beer and ice cream.

My mother is in the lead as we enter the temple. Junko waves me to one side to see something and I double check that the hands I am holding are still those of my children. I notice Mom continue on, but

The main gate to Kyomizu temple.

know that she'll stop in a logical spot and wait for us. The rest of us file past a large metal pole that, surprisingly, proves impossible to lift. For 10 minutes, we watch people being surprised then moving on before we get our turn. We are equally surprised, then move on.

Moments later, we are again surprised: My mother has vanished.

My mother is extremely uncomfortable with heights and none of the three possible directions she might have gone seem probable: A steep staircase upward, a steep staircase downward or the narrow and flimsy-looking bridge crossing to the rest of the gardens. Still, I am not worried. She's not a three-year-old. In fact, she's an unusually healthy Canadian specimen and I judge that it would take five men to take her down, in a kidnapping. Also, I think it's so obvious that we don't come from money that everyone knew it the moment we stepped off the city bus.

As I sit waiting with two extremely bored children, I realize that I have made a critical error in allowing my wife and father to carry out the search together. My father will immediately switch into "Man of Action" mode and Junko, being Japanese, would pole vault over a speed bump. Moments later, I hear an announcement over the loudspeakers: "Blah, blah, blah, blah, blah Mrs. Dean." Its barely audible, but having had time to think it through, I am expecting it.

The National Guard cannot be far behind. Allowed to continue without restraint, my wife and father have a good chance of finding Malaysia Airlines Flight 370 and Amelia Earhart before they stumble upon my mother. I briefly consider the benefits to all of mankind, but Dad and Junko have been gone so long that both children have to pee. I don't want to hear my name over the loudspeakers or see myself on the evening news but I am forced to move toward the bathrooms. Luckily, we bump into Junko on the way. She tells me that Dad has gone back to the restaurant where we had ice cream. It was the place we all agreed to meet, if we got separated.

I lead Junko down the garden path—for the second time, her father might say. I still see no reason to worry and I'm sure we'll stumble across my mother. Sure enough, Mom's found herself a relatively comfortable rock at the park exit and is busy smiling and refusing help from every attendant that passes, as well as the mumbling man we'd seen begging for change.

As it happens, this location is twenty feet from our agreed-upon meeting place. I scan the crowd and see everyone except my father. Now, it's my father who's missing.

We wait and bow to well wishers who have been alerted to the emergency and are glad that things have worked out for the best. What the worst might possibly have been, I cannot guess.

Fifteen minutes later, Dad appears. From his point of view, he has rescued us all.

Mumbling man stands passively chanting for hours, ever ready for donations to the shrine.

CHAPTER 17

Welcome to Rural Japan

Day 7: Mon, April 20th

Today we embark on the last leg of our 10-day journey. We're leaving Kyoto by Bullet Train, heading back to Tokyo where we'll board a train bound for Junko's hometown of Fukaya. We're expecting her brother to meet us there with his large van.

Junko's a bit nervous about missing our Bullet Train, so after a leisurely breakfast, and with nothing else to do, we arrive at the station at noon; two hours early.

Mom and Dad do puzzles and I set the kids up, watching a movie on the laptop. I brought it so that I can write, but I think I'm happier that it can show movies.

I people-watch and realize that Junko could be making money offering advice to the confused caucasian tourists who wander like dazed ghosts, probably looking for a decent coffee and a donut.

It's seven p.m. by the time we arrive at Fukaya Station, where we are warmly greeted by Junko's father and sister-in-law, as well as her brother. At first, I am flattered by the turnout, but then they explain that Junko's brother sold his van and so they needed three of their diminutive cars to transport us all.

In my father-in-law's car, on the way out of the station, Dad spots McDonald's, which ends up being our first meal at Junko's family home.

In an earnest attempt to provide my mother and father maximum privacy, the family has cleared the spare room for them—behind walls that are paper thin, as they are made of paper. Also, there are holes in the paper. They have thoughtfully provided my mother a foldout bed to make it easier for her to get in and out of bed. Dad sleeps on a futon, like the rest of us.

By Western standards, it seems sparse and authentically Japanese, and a far cry from the luxury in which we were swaddled, less than 12 hours ago.

A little too late, I am beginning to see my father-in-law's house through the eyes of my parents.

The Household:

Ok, knit your brow for a few paragraphs, because I want to give you the lay of the land, and this will involve describing the relationships and the atmosphere in my father-in-law's house.

My father-in-law is known to my family as "Jisan" because that is how the kids used to mispronounce the Japanese word for Grandfather (Ojiisan), when they were younger. Ok, ok... it was me who mispronounced it. Jisan is about 75 and a bachelor, having lost his wife about 10 years ago.

Jisan's house has two floors; each a complete home. As is tradition among most Japanese, the eldest son (Katsuya) lives upstairs

with his wife (Teruyo) and their two children (Kazuki, 21 and Hiroki, 18.) The eldest son usually inherits the father's estate, so Katsuya is being groomed to take over the family's farming business. My wife, Junko, is a few years younger than Katsuya and is Jisan's only other child. Kazuki has a girlfriend named Ayane who is a frequent guest.

Including my mother, father, our two kids and myself, there are now 12 people contained in a 2000 sqft. paper box, for the next three days. Should be fun!

The house is traditional in style and sits in the center of a large yard, surrounded by a high, cement fence. Inside the house, the walls are sliding panels of paper. Such distinctions between inside and outside—strangers and family, others and self—lie at the core of many aspects of Japanese culture. In terms of privacy, Japanese are comfortable to experience it only within their thoughts. This is one of the major differences between the comfort zones of the Japanese and those of my mother.

Outside it looks pristine, but inside, Jisan's house is not the 5-star accommodation it once was. Fifteen years ago, when I first visited, the perfection of each room was impressive, but he had a wife taking care of the household details, back then. Now there are holes in the paper walls, peeling wallpaper, broken doors on the kitchen cabinets and sliding doors that grind instead of glide.

As most of the walls slide and all the doors are extremely thin, everything rattles and echoes throughout the house, when moved. There is no sneaking to the bathroom at 3am. As a consequence, the Japanese members of the family sleep very deeply while the Canadians lie awake, either hearing or making strange sounds in the night.

With 12 people coming and going, there is not a quiet minute or private space. My wife's family share limited space without apparent need for elbow room or stealth. In fact, they seem to love noise. No sooner does someone enter the house than they turn on one of the many TV's, for background noise. Contributing to the cacophony, the young adults love playing with our kids, which ratchets their volume knobs to eleven.

If you add to all of this confusion the inability to communicate, it's very disorienting for Canadian visitors. In doing their son the favor of traveling to this strange land, my parents have stepped 8,000 miles outside their comfort zone. At this moment, looking at the two of them struggling to maintain a pleasant facade, I have never had more sympathy for anyone than I do for myself. It's now obvious to me that the crazy things children ask of their parents, never ends.

My Japanese has improved since my last visit *(how could it not?)* and I now have some ability to communicate and understand what is going on and so, for the first time, I find myself quite relaxed in Jisan's home and excited to express my many profound thoughts and opinions. Their smiles tell me that they are impressed.

Later that night, after we have all settled in to our beds, we hear Jisan repeatedly calling out in his sleep: *"Zen zen Chigau!"*

ME: What's he saying?

NOAH: Dad, it's the same thing he's been saying to you, all day: *"That's completely wrong!"*

CHAPTER 18

Another Day in Fukaya

Day 8: Tues, April 21st

As I've mentioned, Dad is not one for sitting around and so, at 5:30 in the morning, he spontaneously decides to go for a 40-minute jog. When he returns, he locks the front door. Problem is, by that time, Jisan is out and about.

Junko and I are awakened at 6:30 by her father calling her name, from outside.

If this trip has taught me nothing else, it has taught me that a good, comfortable breakfast is the foundation of a happy crew of tourists. Recalling my habits from our last visit, five years ago, Teruyo has stocked the kitchen with bread, butter, jam, coffee and breakfast cereals—items that they would not otherwise buy. But because Japanese cuisine is markedly different than Canadian, there are exactly two knives in the house. I notice this while hacking at a loaf of bread with a butter spreader. For breakfast, I serve my Mom and Dad a mangled piece of dry toast and instant coffee.

Junko's single biggest failure in planning this trip has been in securing the cooperation of the weather. We now realize just how much all of our plans and arrangements hinge on decent weather.

Most Japanese homes, including this one, do not have central heating. The weather has deteriorated and so it's a bracing 14°C (57°F), inside the house. Thank god the toilet seat is heated. It's probably where Mom and Dad would prefer to spend the day.

I discuss my parents' accommodation with Jisan who reckons that they should be comfortable here as the weather is roughly the same as in Victoria, this time of year. I point out that, in Canada, we do not have weather inside our houses. Jisan suddenly "gets it," fishes an electric heater from a closet and plugs it in, in my parents' room.

The rain stops and the day becomes warm enough for us to go for a walk around the neighborhood. At last, Japan delivers some of the serenity that I had promised my mother. Dad's more of a "Do-er" and doesn't really appreciate serenity, obviously having forgotten his days of child-rearing.

As we walk, a van decorated with signs meanders through the neighborhood. Some very enthusiastic person inside is babbling, via megaphones affixed to the roof. There is a civic election going on and vehicles like this will visit us about twice a day, for the next week. The first time I saw one of these, I ran after it for three blocks before realizing it wasn't selling ice cream. I just couldn't imagine anyone being so enthusiastic about a thing, if it wasn't ice cream.

Noticing that my parent's haven't eaten anything substantial in 24 hours, Jisan takes us all to a steak house for dinner. My parent's are happy, though my children are chomping at the bit to get some authentic Japanese sushi.

One thing I know about visiting Jisan's house is that you never have any idea what will happen next. You may go to bed agreeing it would be good to wake up late and read a good book only to be

roused for a road trip to an ancient shrine or modern shopping mall; whatever they've determined you will enjoy. Largely, the determining process happens without consultation. Perhaps, when you arrived you casually said something like, "nice vase," because that was the only Japanese phrase you could muster, and now you find yourself touring a ceramic factory, three hours into the mountains.

We are all still tired from all our exploring and eight days of strangeness but comforted in our belief that we are returning to Jisan's for a leisurely game of Ground Golf. Instead, we find ourselves hijacked and on a two-hour journey to see the garden at Hitsujiyama Park (Hitsujiyama Koen.) One of us must have said "nice flower," at some point. The garden is impressive, even though it's off-season and only half the blossoms are blooming. So, what do you do to justify two hours of driving to a five-minute spectacle? You spend two hours and a hundred dollars in the adjacent tourist shops.

This turns out to be the place we purchase most of our souvenirs *(omiyage)* for people back home.

That night, the eldest son, Kazuki (21) brings his girlfriend, Ayane, home for dinner. Kazuki has always been popular but he is the eldest son of a farmer—destined to be a farmer, himself—and modern women are not generally attracted to the lifestyle of farm-wife, though that lifestyle has changed and is no longer the hardship it once was. Ayane appears to adore Kazuki, seemingly oblivious to any such concerns.

Ayane is not what I expected. Rather than being a delicate flower, like most young

Inside a car parked in a private garage are life-sized cardboard cutouts, presumably of the owners. Neither my wife nor her family or friends can offer any explanation for this one. I thought it might be to discourage thieves, or crows.

Japanese girls I've met; she's athletic, and more tomboyish than dolled up. She's studying to become a nurse and has a part time job as a swimming instructor. I like her.

Ayane can speak quite a bit of English and so we quickly start talking. Most people say that I look deceptively young, but almost immediately, Ayane correctly guesses that I'm 56.

"But sixty is the new forty," she quips. I smile, thinly. For me the logic falls short because, by extension, "dead is the new alive."

I don't like her.

Rihana and Noah enjoy their first sushi meal of the trip.

CHAPTER 19

The End Draws Near

Day 9: Wed, April 22nd

It's Mom and Dad's last full day in Japan, and a very unorganized one; much of it spent listening to those around us scramble to find something for us to do in the rain. The only thing I really want to do—and number one on my Japan to-do list—is to visit an izakaya (neighborhood pub) and have a beer with my parents, in a traditional Japanese setting. There's a great one about a block away. Thinking this was a slam-dunk, I saved this event for when we had nothing better: Like now! Turns out, the local one is no longer popular and not open very often, and, in any case, weirdly, all local izakaya's are closed on Wednesdays.

Jisan is goaded into taking us to a restaurant where we can enjoy deep fried foods and a beer. It's an entirely modern looking restaurant, about an hour's drive away, and none of us really understands why we are there except that this is how things get twisted when the Japanese are trying too hard to please. My wife is unable to come with us and my father-in-law refuses to drink, making the excuse that he has to drive. This is such a sudden departure from the man I've known for 15 years that it makes me wonder if he's hiding a grim secret: Like, that he is dying. I file this away for later. We eat and drink in relative silence and return home.

I used to fight it, but am now used to my Japanese family's persistence in pleasing, which is often based on a misunderstanding and leads to gifts or outings that you really do not welcome. I have learned that if the Japanese offer you something, then they have pretty much already decided that you need it, or at least, that your life would be enhanced with one... or a dozen. Refusing their gestures is a waste of time, energy and your bad Japanese. I know of at least four ways to say "no," in Japanese. They have all proven equally ineffective.

For the rest of the day, Mom reads a book, huddled in her room with a coat on and the heater going, full blast. Dad watches Netflix on the laptop, then a baseball game, on Japanese TV.

This is how my parents endure their final full day in Japan: POW's scratching notches on the wall.

*Father-in-laws watch TV in the Japanese-
style living room.*

CHAPTER 20

End of Days

Day 10: Thu, April 23rd

The family all turn out to accompany Mom and Dad to the bus which will take them to the airport. Dad insists on taking the earliest bus which will deposit them at the terminal at least four hours in advance of their departure. Though none of us can imagine any scenario in which they are unable to navigate their way from the bus to the airplane, we don't argue and I start thinking that this book might get an epilogue with a late-breaking plot twist.

Keeping the *izakaya* experience in mind, I have already checked to make sure that buses run on Thursdays, just in case.

The sun has finally come out and the day is warm and bright. While we wait for the bus, what we believe to be a large hummingbird zooms past and lands on the pavement, a few feet away. Noah is the first to notice that the hummingbird has mandibles and a stinger. Though it's just as large, it's not a hummingbird, but a Japanese Giant Hornet; a three-inch-long wasp.

My father finally breaks. "I want to go home," he says.

The bus appears and we all hug goodbye. As Dad embraces me and shakes my hand, he palms to me an envelope filled with cash. It's an emotional moment and though no words are exchanged, his meaning is clear: "Whatever the cost, bring me back one of those Japanese toilet seats."

They board the bus and it soon pulls away. All involved are simultaneously sad and relieved.

And that's the story of how my mother and father abandoned me in a foreign country.

Post Script:

My parents made it home without issue, but a couple of funny things happened later, that same day.

Though Jisan always appeared happy and nonchalant, I guess he'd been on his best behavior during my parents' visit. At dinner, and for the first time since we arrived, he breaks open a bottle of beer. Good news: He's not dying.

Many Japanese have begun using beds instead of the traditional futons, and it turns out that the folding bed Mom used was actually Hiroki's. He asks for my help to fold it and lug it upstairs to his room. I notice a pin attached to a chain and assumed it's to lock the bed in it's folded position, but we can't figure out how, so we take it, as is. At about 2am there's a thunderous crash from upstairs, as if Fred Flintstone opened his closet and his bowling ball collection came tumbling out. We are awakened at about 6am by a similar noise. We later learn that Hiroki's bed had collapsed twice, during the night. Apparently, the pin was meant to secure the bed in its unfolded position.

During the three days that my mother slept on that bed, the pin was not in place.

CHAPTER 21

Parental Guidance:
(What 10 Days in Japan taught me about my parents.)

• By starting with the attitude that he didn't want to go in the first place and that he would be miserable the entire time, my father was able to appreciate it when something sucked less than he'd expected and so, seemed to cope better than the rest of us. My perpetually optimistic mother, on the other hand, found herself constantly challenged. Hail to the power of negative thinking!

• During our conversations in Kyoto, I learned that my father is capable of deep thoughts. Some of these thoughts have involved him changing his mind. These two observations fly in the face of his family image as an old fashioned, black and white, keep-it-simple kind of man.

• My mother's observations on Japanese culture, my children and relationships within the family were as insightful as I'd imagined they'd be. Her wisdom and ability to offer sage advice, remains unchallenged.

• For my father, I will finally reveal all the reasons I asked them on this trip:

1) When I was 18, my parents took us all to Europe for a month. I wanted to return the favor—although, at times, it may have seem more like retribution than reward. Payback is such a funny word, don't you think?

2) To bring both of my parents closer to my children. This was an experience that none of us are going to forget.

3) So that I could share an adventure with my parents.

4) To connect my family to Japan, which is now a permanent part of my life, and the life of my children.

5) To visit Jisan and connect with his family, as he has visited us and connected with ours.

6) To show them the Japanese toilet.

ABOUT THE AUTHOR

William M. Dean lives in Victoria, BC, Canada with his wife, Junko and their two children, Noah and Rihana. A full biography and more of his work can be found online at wmdean.com and wmdbooks.com.

A MESSAGE FROM THE AUTHOR

You have my heartfelt thanks for purchasing my book. I sincerely hope that it was as entertaining for you to read, as it was for me to live.

I am always open to questions and/or feedback. You can contact me from my webpage at wmdbooks.com, or my blog at wmdean.com.

And, if you can spare a few minutes, a review on Amazon.com, favorable or not, would be helpful to me, as well as to prospective readers.

In the following pages, I have included an excerpt from my novel, *The Space between Thought*. If you enjoy reading this sample, you can find the rest of the novel at wmdbooks.com, amazon.com and other fine book retailers.

A novel of love, life, death, tea and time travel.

William M. Dean

The Space between Thought
A novel of love, life, death, tea and time travel.

Excerpt from Chapter 17:

The helicopter held nine travelers in rows of three, and Paula cursed her luck at having to sit next to the sticklike, well-dressed man to her right. He was some sort of government employee who fancied himself the keystone of a project, which, he mentioned, was of extreme importance—an economic feasibility study on sewage treatment diversification or some such thing. Whatever it was, Paula had not grasped either the name or its significance though she could not help but notice the unhealthy pallor of his skin, the thinning of his coarse red hair, the uneven moustache, and breath that smelled like bad fish. He divided his attention between cell phone and laptop and Paula, blatantly hitting on her whenever he found time. He talked loudly on the phone and never failed to announce to the other party that he was currently helicoptering to Vancouver for an emergency meeting.

The seven other passengers remained still and quiet, undoubtedly sharing similar thoughts.

The pilot was running through a lengthy preflight checklist. On the tarmac, a boarding attendant checked his watch and looked anxiously about for the final passenger: Simon.

The annoying man to her right folded his phone, and Paula checked her own, more to appear busy than to verify Simon's lateness. She was surprised and slightly worried. Simon had not missed an appointment in months, was habitually fifteen minutes early. She was about to make a call when Simon appeared, awkwardly swinging his briefcase, hair and clothing wildly disheveled by the wind as he jogged across the asphalt.

As Simon got settled, the pilot's voice came over the intercom. "Good day and welcome aboard Heli-Link Airways flight 115. This is Captain Lofton and I'll be your pilot for the duration of our thirty-five-minute journey into downtown Vancouver. Unfortunately, we'll be flying through a little turbulence today, so make sure your seatbelts are fastened and securely tightened. Be advised that Canadian Flight and Safety Regulations prohibit the use of personal electrical devices such as cell phones, laptops, and video recorders during takeoff and landing." Paula worried that chatting her up would be the only activity left to the public servant, but he kept on tapping away at the laptop, apparently exempt from such regulations.

Paula heard the ascending whine and felt the rumble through her seat as the powerful turbine engine powered up. One seat over, the government man finally flipped closed the lid on his laptop.

Simon stared out the window as the commuter-helicopter drew away from the pad. Paula stared ahead. He had barely acknowledged her as he boarded. Things were going well for the company but were not as much fun as they used to be. Simon could still be witty and charming, but only if required. When he was not schmoozing, he was all business.

"Business is not a circus. No need for clowns," he'd recently told her.

It was as if the kid in him had died with Celeste. And Simon made a grim adult. From the way he acted since her death, you'd think that he and Celeste had had a fairytale romance. That was far from true, but Paula no longer felt safe enough to be so honest.

She remembered congratulating herself on convincing Simon to visit the psychologist. He went only once but returned to work with renewed vigor, seemingly inspired to move forward. He tackled problems like a kid with a hammer. But his fervor was manic, and Paula soon came to suspect that the inspiration was fear. Something had happened in that session with Fiona Nickle that had frightened Simon so badly that he could not bear to dwell. Now, he was a juggernaut, plowing through a four-month backlog like a tank through a china shop. There were casualties, but a tank has no rearview mirror.

The tank stalled on only one issue: Celeste's memorial fund. Family and friends had organized an arts scholarship in her name, to be administered through UVic. They had generated some funds but hoped the majority would come from Simmersion's corporate sponsorship. Without a significant and ongoing commitment, the scholarship would be nothing more than a one-time gift. Simon shredded letters, sidestepped phone calls, and ducked appointments in order to avoid making the decision. Paula knew that money was not the issue. Did he think that he could will Celeste alive by not acknowledging that she was gone?

The vehicle bounced through turbulence the entire way. The captain's earlier words, " a little turbulence," must have been a euphemism because Paula felt like she was riding a rodeo bull. Though the helicopter's interior was well insulated, the jet turbine engine was loud enough to inhibit conversation. Simon and Paula did not talk.

Eventually, the captain made another announcement. "Ladies and gentlemen, we are approaching Vancouver harbor and will be touching down in approximately five minutes. The weather in Vancouver is eight degrees Celsius with low cloud, rain, and gusty conditions. We'll be coming in low, beneath the clouds, which should allow for a nice view of the Lions Gate Bridge. Please continue to heed the warning lights and keep your safety belts fastened until the rotors have come to a complete stop. Passengers planning to return to Victoria later today, be advised that due to weather conditions, all flights have been canceled until further notice. Thank you."

Paula and Simon exchanged a glance, and the man to her right flipped open his cell phone. The pilot was too busy to notice.

As promised, when the copter broke from the clouds, the Lions Gate Bridge was close ahead. As they passed over, the wind seemed to drop from beneath the blades for just a second, and the copter plunged fifty feet. The commuters gasped as one and became unsettled when the pilot offered no assurances. Paula peered forward into the cockpit. The copilot was flipping through a set of laminated cards, reading bits and pieces to the pilot, who seemed calm but focused.

On the heliport tarmac, landing lights winked, poking bright pinpoints through the gray veil of dusk. A man in a blue-and-white windbreaker waved a red flashlight while talking into a walkie-talkie. At the edge of the landing circle, another man stood dressed in a fluorescent-yellow rain slicker, though it was not raining. Ominously, he held a fire hose.

The pitch of the turbine rose and the copter hovered above the target, tilting and bobbing like a cork while the pilot tried to gauge the wind to find a column of steady air in which to descend.

William M. Dean

The government man's computer beeped then went black, and he swapped the battery for his spare. Making it fit was a bit of a trick in the tight quarters, and he fiddled with it for some time. After it was installed, he didn't seem happy with its performance. From time to time, the unit would ping in soft complaint, and the man would jostle or knock at the battery compartment until things got right.

Many minutes later, the pilot's patience seemed to pay off. The wind abated and held steady. Paula heard the engine's pitch descending, saw the large, white H draw closer.

A gust caught the tail and spun the helicopter around. Paula grabbed her cross, pressed her fist against her chest. The pilot seemed unconcerned, continued studying his gauges and the ground through a triangular window near his feet.

The government man was oblivious to the tension, absorbed in some detail on his laptop. His screen dimmed, and he banged the housing impatiently. As the copter came within safe jumping distance of the tarmac, the anxiety in the cabin evaporated, and someone let out a mild cheer.

Paula noticed Simon reaching for his briefcase when the laptop beeped for the final time. The screen's image winked and wobbled at the edges, and the machine uttered a strangled note. The stick man rapped knobby knuckles against the plastic, and the battery dislodged. He fumbled for it, but it slid along his trousers and fell to the floor between his knees. He clawed after it, desperately, perhaps dimly sensing that the situation was strangely mutating.

A thousandth of a second later, there was a whiplike crack and a small arc of blue as the terminals shorted across a metal bolt.

Twenty feet from the ground, the gauges on the instrument panel fluctuated then died. There was no time for the startled pilot to react. The wind battered vehicle dipped, and the blades gouged the pavement and shattered. The impact slammed the travelers forward. Seats ripped free of their bolts, loose objects became bullets, and both pilots were smashed against the glass, leaving angry smudges. The corner of his laptop carved a gash in the government man's face, digging out most of his left eye. His scream was short, for an instant later, a shard of glass ripped through his throat, ending his pain and freeing up his tight schedule for eternity.

122

But the ride was far from over. The spin of the engine slapped the aluminum frame sideways against the asphalt, and shrapnel strafed the area. An instant later, the scrap of fuselage summersaulted across the pad. Blacktop filled the cockpit windshield then burst through like water into a bathysphere, instantly pulverizing the cockpit and everything within. Then the engine exploded. The frame buckled, and the cabin came apart as if it were unmaking itself.

*** *** ***

Simon caught flashes of Paula's terror-stricken face, gray sky, rag-dolls, blood, glass—a blurred collage flipping by him like a hundred frames from a hundred horror films. Rending metal screamed, and the explosion roared around him. A collision of gyrating forces tore and pounded, pulled and crushed him against his seat. He could make sense of none of it.

Simon's chair was suddenly blown from the wreckage. He tried to scream, but the air had been punched from his lungs. He flailed and waited silently for impact and death.

*** *** ***

Abruptly, there was silence and calm. It's over. I'm dead, he thought.

Simon drifted unmoving for a long time. What hurry was there in death? But then sensation eased back into him like motion in a great clock; small wheels spinning quietly, meshing into larger upon larger wheels, until finally a cacophony of movement and the bonging of massive chimes.

Cold! Wet!

Simon opened his eyes, had to close them against the salt of the sea. The passenger seats were purposely designed to float. He felt the buckle across his lap and realized that he was hanging upside down in the water.

Simon's nerves came fully conscious, and he felt fangs of pain down his left arm and across his chest. He was alive and drowning. He choked on seawater and scraped frantically at the buckle. The snap released, but, unexpectedly, he did not float free of the chair. He did not stop to analyze. His lungs were screaming, and his one thought was to find the surface. He flailed and kicked and somehow managed to pull himself across the chair and scramble to the surface. He lay draped across the backrest, exhausted, eyes closed, gasping like a landed salmon.

He was seriously injured, he decided, because he could not entirely satisfy his lungs. Each breath seemed an effort, the amount of air he drew, insufficient. He still felt he was drowning, though much more slowly now. He knew that on the pier above there must be bedlam—screaming victims, shouting rescuers, perhaps sirens. He heard none of it, and so presumed his eardrums had been punctured.

Would they think to look for him in the water? With some effort, Simon opened his eyes. Thankfully, a metal ladder hung from the pier, only a few feet away. He almost cried with relief. But then, something struck him so odd that all emotion drained away. He lifted his head, looked around, took stock for the first time. His shortness of breath and the stabbing of his wounds became remote.

There was no wind, not a wisp. The waves were still. Completely still. Rock solidly still.

He heard his own gasp of surprise. It sounded oddly distorted, but he was not deaf—not entirely, at least. Experimentally, he tapped at the molded plastic of his makeshift life raft. The sound came back unnaturally deep and died quickly, like a shout in snowfall. When he looked down, he saw water running off his body, but slowly, like clear honey. The sea was as still as a photo, so the helicopter chair was also still. He grabbed the headrest and yanked, expecting it to roll beneath him. It resisted, moving only a fraction and with glacier-like slowness.

Simon looked again in all directions but could see no movement. Of course, from his position, the view was limited.

A shot of fear coursed through him, and he jumped toward the ladder, earth, safety. The frozen chair was a stable platform, and he had no difficulty traversing the distance. He fell against the lowest rung and scrambled upward. Halfway, he dared look back. His path was blazed by a trail of splash marks and water droplets. Beneath his left elbow, the most recent drop hung, suspended in mid air. He touched it with a finger. It felt like syrup, deformed appropriately, shifted slightly in position, remained hanging.

At the top of the ladder Simon stopped, transfixed, only the top of his head peeking above the deck planks. Before him was a static diorama of the helicopter accident: a perfect holograph. Someone had stopped the projector of life to give Simon a private screening.

Behind the heliport, the backdrop of rail yard, overpasses, and the high-rises all seemed normal. Over a million souls occupied midtown Vancouver on any given day, and Simon was startled at how the city consumed them so that a bustling hive of activity could appear completely still without seeming abnormal. The landscape was dotted with vehicles, but from this distance, it was impossible to tell if they should have been moving, or were parked. The only person was propped against the railing of a road that crossed above the rail yard. The figure was still, but might have been resting or taking in the view. In the clear space between two buildings, Simon noticed a loose formation of indistinct dots. He squinted and realized that they were pigeons suspended in midflight. You just had to know what to look for. To the right, the tall bright banners of Canada Place were billowed and still. To the left, a thin cylinder of dirty smoke poked from a factory like the straw in a tropical drink, as inanimate as the wind that bent it.

Maybe he really was dead.

But he was cold, felt pain, felt the urge to breathe, was breathing. That did not seem like death.

When he had gathered sufficient strength and courage, Simon stepped into the tableau. He was cautious as he approached the litter of wreckage suspended in midflight. If God shouted "Action!" he would instantly be impaled or diced. A small, distorted nut hung before him, at the edge of the explosion. He examined it from all angles, tried to push it out of his way. It was warm, bordering on hot, and would not budge. He pushed harder without success, then put the shoulder of his tattered jacket to it. It remained stationary. Simon ducked under and weaved his way into the heart of the event. He had to find Paula.

The wreck was balanced on its nose in a way that made it obvious that it had not yet come to rest. A fan of sparks glowed statically where metal met ground. As he neared, he found it difficult to push forward. A cloud of small particles enveloped him in warmth and resisted his movement through them. It was like walking neck-deep in mud. And, he was finding it increasingly difficult to draw breath.

Simon accidentally collided with a spray of oil. Nearer the wreck, flame was creeping up the spray. Black droplets flattened against his chest but did not absorb into the fabric of his shirt. He flicked them off, and they atomized into a finer cloud of spatter. There was a thick smoke, but instead of billowing in plumes, it radiated outward in inky ribbons, streaming from cracks and holes. When he batted at them, they moved aside and separated in slow motion. He peered through a mangled window.

It was horrifying. A woman's face was covered in bright flames, her hands blackened and clawing. The man next to her was tucked between the seats ahead, folded backward like a dollar bill in a money clip. His seat belt had either snapped or come unbolted. Charred and twisted remnants stood like a frozen flag. The man in Simon's row was probably dead, his body helixed like seaweed by the torque. A volcano of juicy flesh had erupted behind his left ear. Some of the passengers were obscured from his view by loose or collapsed chairs and wall panels. Others, like Paula, were missing.

Simon looked out a gaping hole in the far wall, the one that he had been tossed through. Paula and he had been seated next to each other, and both chairs were missing. It made sense that she might have been tossed toward the harbor. Through the hole he saw a tangle of limbs in a business suit skidding along the pavement. Not Paula, but she was out there somewhere.

Perhaps in the harbor. Simon navigated around the crumpling ball of metal. From this angle, he could see the pilot's ragged torso dangling from the shattered windshield, his head at an unnatural angle and pinned beneath the nose.

Simon turned and spotted a large section of the cabin floating near the edge of the wharf. Paula's chair was still firmly bolted to it, and she hung, strapped into the chair. Her eyes were saucers staring into her trajectory. He followed her unseeing gaze. She was about eight feet away from a lamp encased in a dome-shaped grid of thick metal, heading straight for it. The outcome was as clear now as it would be later. The lamp would make mush of her skull.

She was suspended almost upside down, six feet off the ground. He reached up and touched her face. It felt like plastic, and, as he expected, she did not react. He brushed hair from her open mouth. It was heavy and bristlelike. He pried at the latch of her seatbelt, but it was like trying to undo the buckle on a bronze statue. One of her shoes was slipping off. Simon managed to push it back on, but it was a major effort.

He stepped away. Was there no more he could do than pull back her hair and replace a shoe? Of all the things he had come to expect of this bizarre experience, the least of those was a magnified view of Paula's death. And what was the point of that? What was her mighty God's purpose in granting him access to an instant without the power to alter it?

Simon felt a wave of dizziness and a noise like the crash of gargantuan cymbals erupted around him. Instinctively, he ducked to the asphalt: crouched there, panting, eyes darting expectantly.

All still. All silent.

But things had changed. When he rose again to examine Paula, he noticed that she had moved. She was now less than five feet from the lamp and certain death.

There had to be a way to change that.

He tried to stay clear of the storm of metal as he toured the heliport. He had to work quickly. There was no telling how long this phenomenon would last. Somewhere there had to be a tool, something that he could use to remove the lamp from Paula's path. He found a large pipe, but when he lifted it, he discovered that it weighed several times what he'd expected—too much to be an effective sledgehammer. When he let go of it, it took several seconds to drop to the ground.

Simon did not dwell.

The frozen figure in the yellow slicker had dropped the hose and started running away half crouched, hands shielding his head. Simon ignored him but followed the canvas snake to a heavy-duty brass faucet. Above it, where he hoped would be an axe, he found only a painted outline, the shadow of a solution. Beneath that, thirty feet of folded fire hose.

With some effort, he pushed through the glass doors of the terminal looking for more tools; perhaps he could find the missing axe or a hacksaw. Inside, office workers posed like horror-struck mannequins. A coffee had been caught in midslop, about to decorate a woman's blouse and paperwork. A glass vase was toppling from a shelf. Two men were balanced like a pair of discus throwers as they bolted for the door. The first man had just tossed the second a blue-and-white windbreaker, and it floated between them. Simon was suddenly reminded of the fire and ice spell in Arcane Empire.

The flicker of neon made him consider the lights. Looking across the ceiling, he saw that some were brightly lit, others dim, the remainder dark. As he watched, the pattern changed. His heart raced. Time was not completely suspended. Neon lights, he remembered, pulsated at sixty cycles per second. If that was so, then each flicker represented a 120th of a second, about the time it took to expose a snapshot. It gave him a gauge for the remainder of Paula's life. She would be dead in less than a hundred flickers.

Near the back door, Simon found a large, red plywood cabinet with the words "Emergency Tool Kit" stenciled in black. A man stood before it, the lock in his hands. Had there been a key, Simon might have been able to turn it, but the man held a combination lock. Getting into that cabinet was as large a problem as getting rid of the lamp.

Simon growled in frustration, but it came to his ears like the muffled bleat of some animal. He realized that sound did not carry because sound was air in motion, and there was little motion here.

The lights flickered again. He needed another approach.

Back out on the tarmac, the progress of time was clear. The wreck had rotated several degrees, and the pattern of sparks, oil spray, and flying debris had grown. Paula was now four feet from the lamp.

Simon was desperate. Whether real-time suddenly kicked in or not, if he didn't find a solution quickly, he was doomed to witness Paula's death, knowing that he had failed to rescue her. And if time did not resume full speed, it would happen in agonizingly slow motion.

The fire hose leapt to mind. It was a desperate plan at best, but he could come up with something better afterward, if he had the time.

Suspended in time, the heavy-duty canvas fire hose was not as flexible as he might have wished, but he was thankful that it had not yet filled with water. As it was, it kinked and twisted and weighed a ton, and Simon had to use all of his strength to drag it across the helipad.

He could not tie a tight knot with the unwieldy tether, so when he got to Paula, he made several loops around the legs of her chair, and then he twisted it back along itself until he ran out of hose. He examined his work, making certain that the hose was connected in such a way that it would tend to land the chair on its back. At the other end, he inspected the hefty water main and decided that the industrial brass coupling made a secure anchor.

Simon retrieved the length of pipe that he had earlier discarded. There could be no more than three feet of slack in the hose; otherwise Paula might still hit the lamp. Where the hose dipped to the ground, Simon twisted it around the bar. He turned the bar, which twisted the hose, taking up slack with each rotation. Even with the leverage gained using the three-foot pipe, it took all of his muscle to get the hose tight enough to hang above the ground. When the tension mounted beyond his strength, he cautiously let go of the rod. As anticipated, the arrangement started to unwind, but very, very slowly. The bar traveled round, like the second hand on a clock. For once, the physical laws of this strange universe would work for him, instead of against.

He grabbed the bar intending to tighten it back. He managed to stop its rotation but could not move it backward. Simon realized that as the time inched forward, Paula moved forward, tightening the hose and forcing the pipe to spin. He could fight it but could not entirely halt the unwinding. It was all a matter of timing now. If the tension in the hose was released before Paula's flight was arrested, then she was dead.

The pressure of the bar mounted against his shoulder. Simon groaned and shoved, focusing every iota of strength into the effort. He was not as youthful or athletic as he had once been, and the effects of a sedentary lifestyle were immediate. Psychedelic dots appeared at the periphery of his vision. He flushed, and perspiration formed like dew.

There was a blinding flash, and the cosmic cymbals crashed again.

The bar spun twice around, banging Simon's bicep, grazing his temple, and sending him stumbling backward. He grabbed his arm and bellowed an echoless rant that attenuated as fast as if he were screaming into a pillow. His arm throbbed, and he couldn't move his fingers. Probably broken, he guessed. He felt nauseous.

Flash! Crash!

Time leapt forward, and Simon discovered just how vulnerable he was, standing within the plume of an explosion. He felt a searing heat across his right cheek. A razor-like shard of metal had spun past, halted now, inches from his nose.

Time was coming back online, and he had to find a safe place. Instinctively, he headed toward the water. He would be safe on the ladder, below the level of the helipad.

But, as he jogged toward safety, his heart seemed lethargic, and scintillating dots of light and dark began to intrude. Ducking under the hose took an inordinate amount of effort, and he was puffing, staggering, and stumbling by the time he reached the metal ladder.

The thunderous cacophony resumed with a boom, and Simon was blown from the wharf into the churning sea.

Discover more of William's work at:
www.wmdbooks.com

Also, available at
www.amazon.com
and other fine book retailers.

Made in the USA
Lexington, KY
04 April 2016